Captain Clever

Englisch

4. Klasse

Katrin Dreßler

Sonderausgabe

Illustrationen Captain Clever: Franz Gerg
Illustrationen: Doris Oppenauer
Gestaltung: Axel Ganguin
Umschlaggestaltung: Bettina Weisl

ISBN 978-3-8174-6659-7
5166595

Ahoi, ihr Landratten!

Ich bin Captain Clever, ein mutiger und schlauer Pirat. Gemeinsam mit meiner Crew unternehme ich viele aufregende Fahrten. Damit alles glattgeht, muss ich eine Menge Fremdsprachen kennen. Willst du nicht bei mir anheuern und mit mir Englisch lernen?

Mithilfe der spannenden Übungen kannst du den kompletten Englisch-Stoff der vierten Klasse trainieren. Blaue Regelkästen rufen dir wichtige Lerninhalte in Erinnerung. Damit du die Aufgaben erfolgreich lösen kannst, habe ich dir clevere Tipps für dein tägliches Lernen in die gelben Regelkästen geschrieben. Auf den Seiten „Check your English" kannst du den Lernstoff der vorangegangenen Kapitel noch einmal zusammengefasst üben. Deine Lösungen kannst du am Ende des Heftes kontrollieren.

Zwischendurch habe ich dir immer wieder Rätselseiten eingestreut. Hier kannst du deine Konzentrationsfähigkeit verbessern und Spaß machen sie außerdem.

Volle Kraft voraus!

Inhalt

1. Aufgabe

Captain Clever liebt Farben und mag es gerne bunt.
Male ihm einen Regenbogen! Draw a rainbow!

Tipp

Wenn Du nicht weißt, in welcher Reihenfolge die Farben eines Regenbogens strahlen, dann lies das Gedicht von unten nach oben!

2. Aufgabe

Captain Clever mag auch Zahlen recht gerne. Male sie ihm bunt an!
Paint the numbers!

Paint number fifteen grey.

Paint number ninety-nine blue.

Number forty-seven is pink.

Paint number thirty yellow.

Number fifty-five is red.

Number one hundred is brown.

Number thirteen is purple.

Paint number eighty-nine green.

Paint number seventy-two black.

3. Aufgabe

Folge den Zahlen! Was kann Captain Clever durch sein Fernglas sehen? Follow these numbers!

one – nine – twelve – thirteen – fifteen – eighteen – nineteen – twenty-six – thirty – thirty-three – fifteen – thirty-nine – forty – forty-three – fifty – fifty-eight – sixty – twenty-six – sixty-two – seventy-one – seventy-nine – eighty-two – eighty-three – eighty-five – ninety-two – sixty-two – ninety-three – ninety-nine – one

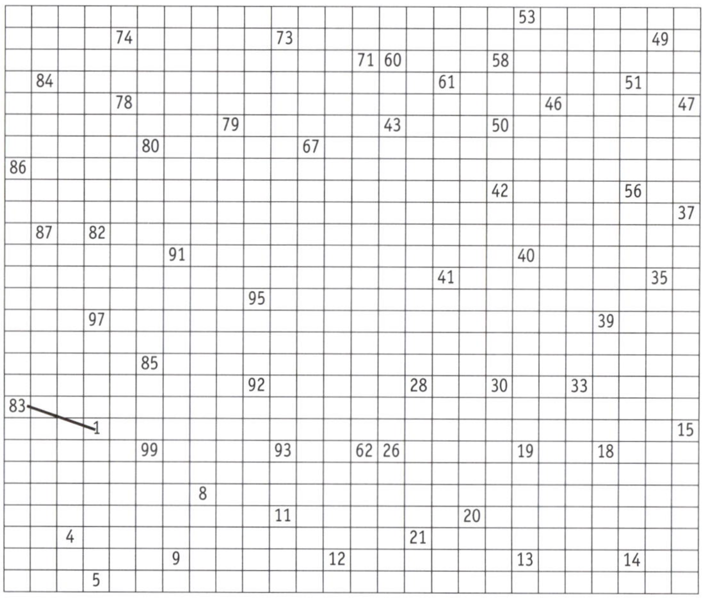

Denke daran!

three = 3
thirteen = 13
thirty = 30

four = 4
fourteen = 14
forty = 40

five = 5
fifteen = 15
fifty = 50

Erinnere dich!

Einer und Zehner werden mit Bindestrich geschrieben:
sixty-one

4. Aufgabe

Captain Clever möchte mit dir ein lustiges Muschelspiel spielen. Vervollständige jede Muschel! Write the numbers!

5. Aufgabe

Hi, ihr Landratten, da bin ich wieder! Das alles gehört zu mir. Was ist was? Verbinde! Draw lines!

grey trousers

an eye patch

a rapier

a pirate ship

an earring

jolly roger (pirate flag)

a treasure map

a red headscarf

a treasure chest

a brown belt

field glasses

a blue coat

an island

a green parrot

6. Aufgabe

Sieh noch einmal genau hin. Was hat Captain Clever, was hat er nicht? Read and put down the right answer!

Captain Clever has got ...

	True	False
... a pirate ship.	x	
... shoes.		
... grey trousers.		
... a green parrot.		
... a yellow T-shirt.		
... a treasure chest.		
... a blue hat.		
... a house.		
... an earring.		
... a pirate flag.		

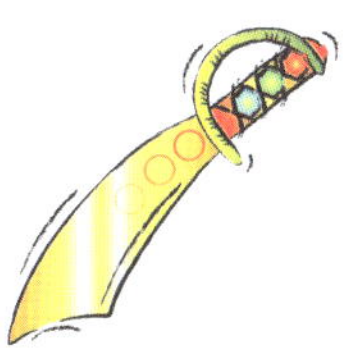

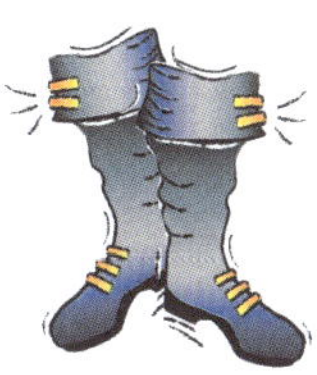

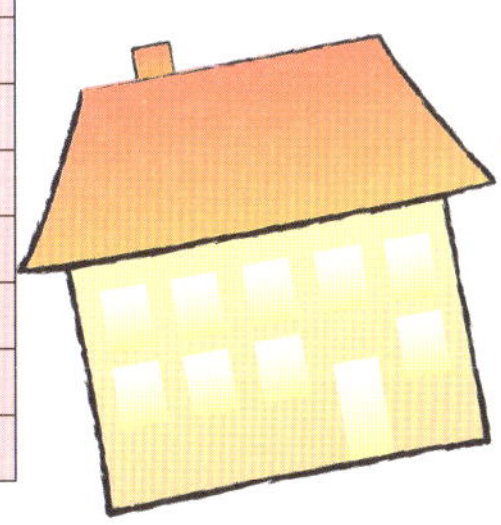

Denke daran!

have got = haben, besitzen
he has got = er hat, er besitzt

7. Aufgabe

Erinnere dich!
Fragst du, sprichst du so:
Has he got ...?
Antwortest du, sprichst du so:
He has got ...

What has Captain Clever got? Read and circle the right answer!

Has he got a parrot?	Yes, he has.	No, he hasn't.
Has he got a ship?	Yes, he has.	No, he hasn't.
Has he got an earring?	Yes, he has.	No, he hasn't.
Has he got shoes?	Yes, he has.	No, he hasn't.
Has he got a treasure map?	Yes, he has.	No, he hasn't.
Has he got a house?	Yes, he has.	No, he hasn't.

Was möchtest du wissen? Stelle jetzt eigene Fragen!

Has he got ______________________?

H________________________________?

H________________________________?

8. Aufgabe

Captain Clever hat von einem Matrosen gelernt, dass auch im Englischen in Einzahl und Mehrzahl unterschieden wird. Übe mit ihm und schreibe zu jedem Wort die Mehrzahl auf!

Denke daran!
Die regelmäßige Mehrzahl wird mit dem Wort und einem hinzugefügten **-s** gebildet.

ship	+s	
apple	+s	
duck	+s	
flower	+s	
basket	+s	
rabbit	+s	
map	+s	

Fruit and vegetables

9. Aufgabe

1. 

2. 

Captain Clever möchte auf große Fahrt gehen und belädt sein Schiff mit viel Obst und Gemüse. Schreibe unter jede Frucht den Namen! Die Buchstabenzeile unter den Bildern hilft dir dabei!

3. 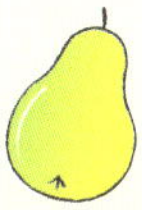

4. 

5. 

6. 

7. 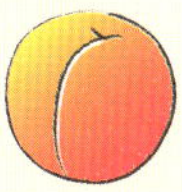

8. 

9. 

10. 

11. 

12. 

18. 

13. 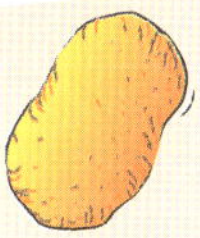

14. 

16. 

17. 

20. 

15. 

19. 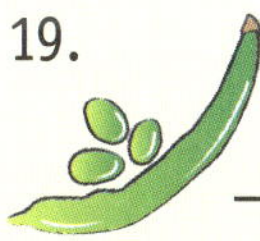

10. Aufgabe

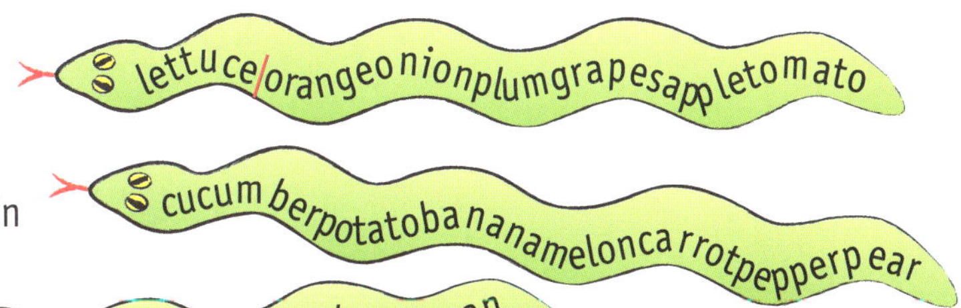

Obst oder Gemüse? Fruit or vegetables? Hilf Captain Clever beim Sortieren!

Fruit

Vegetables

lettuce

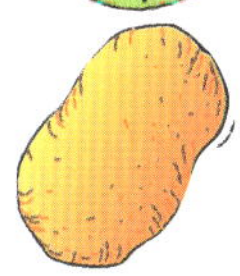

Fruit and vegetables

11. Aufgabe

Captain Clever prüft die Vorratskammer. In riesigen Kisten und Körben sind Obst und Gemüse eingeordnet. Schreibe auf, was es gibt! There is ... / There are ...

Tipp

There is, there is ... nur eines ist's. There are, there are, viele sind's, ist doch klar!

There are bananas.

________________ apples.

________________ onions.

________________ a melon.

________________ oranges.

________________ a pumpkin.

________________ cucumbers.

________________ a pepper.

________________ a pear.

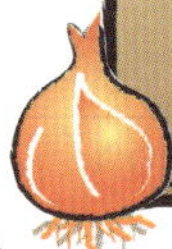

Erinnere dich!

Einzahl – ein **a**, **an** oder **one** steht davor!
Mehrzahl – das Wort hat meistens ein **s** am Ende!

12. Aufgabe

Captain Clever weiß, wie wichtig Lebensmittel für die Reise sind. Er will genau wissen, was da ist und fragt: Was ist an Bord des Schiffes? Sind dort ...? Are there ...?

Tipp

Wenn Du mit **no** (nein) antwortest, endest Du auch mit **not** (nicht)!
No, there are not.
No, there is not.

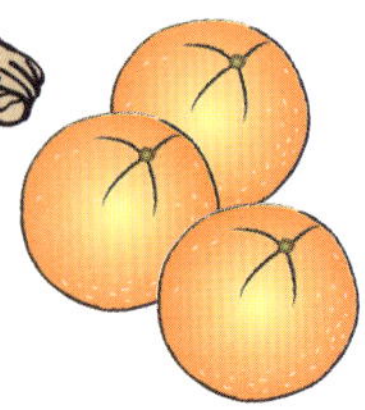

Are there apples?	Yes, there are.
____________ potatoes?	No, there are not.
____________ oranges?	Yes, ________________
____________ lemons?	No, ________________
____________ pears?	Yes, ________________
____________ onions?	No, ________________

Gleiche suchen

Zwei Kronen sind farblich und der Form nach identisch.
Welche sind es?

Punktebild

Verbinde die Punkte den einzelnen Zahlen nach und du wirst ein bestimmtes Transportmittel erkennen!

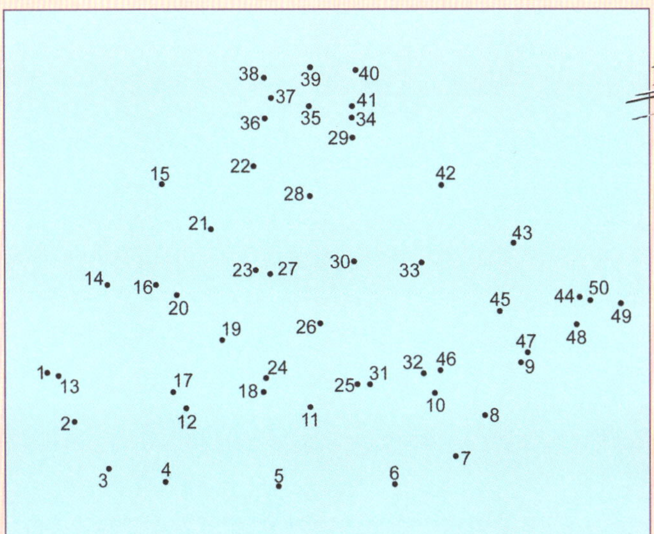

The human body

tongue · neck · bottom · hand · foot · head · lips · eye · knee · toe · shoulder · chest · elbow · leg · hair · back · belly · arm · mouth · tooth · face · ear · finger · nose

13. Aufgabe

Endlich ist alles an Bord! Kein Wunder, dass alle vor Freude strahlen. Beim Einladen der Waren haben sich alle angestrengt und mit ihrem Körper gearbeitet. Welche Teile des Körpers kennst du? Ordne zu!

Denke daran!

Bei manchen Wörtern wird die Mehrzahl unregelmäßig gebildet:
one tooth – two teeth
one foot – two feet

14. Aufgabe

Drei Wörter aus Aufgabe 13 sind nicht zugeordnet worden. Ordne sie hier ein! Fill them in here!

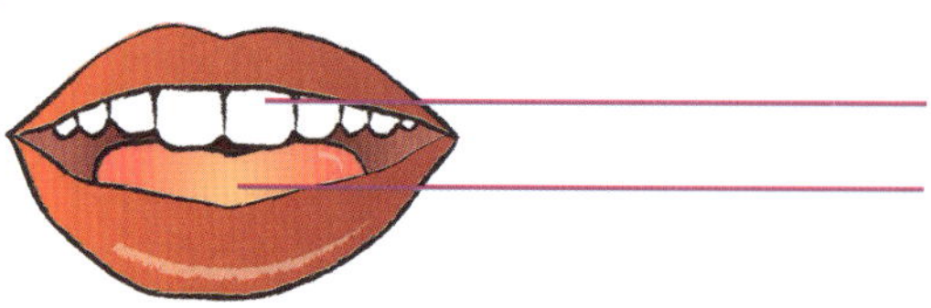

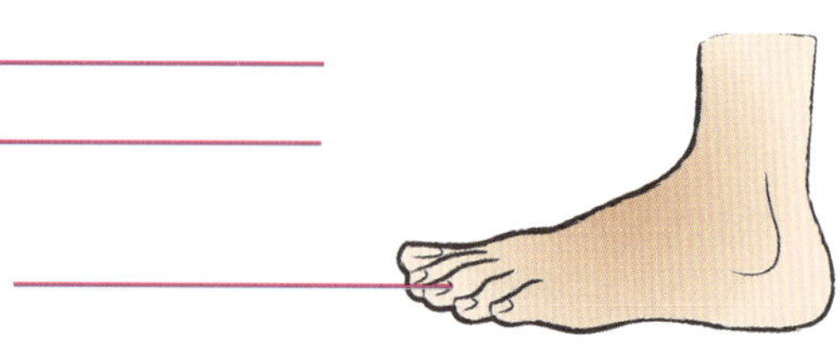

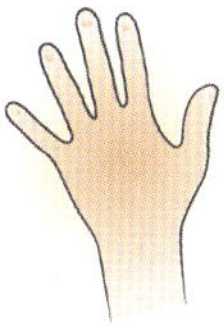

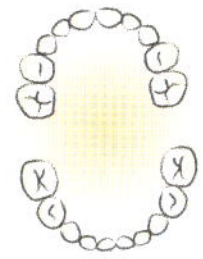

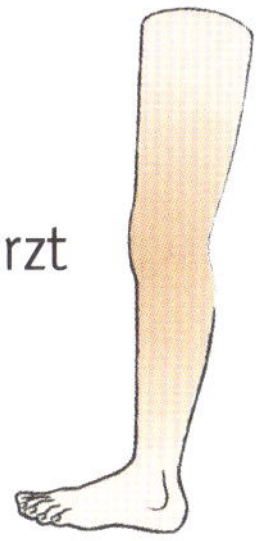

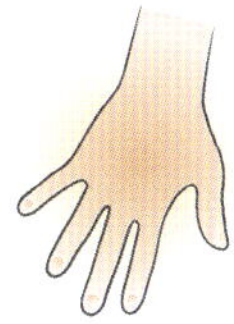

15. Aufgabe

Aua, das tut weh. Ouch, that hurts. Captain Clever ist gestürzt und hat sich verletzt. Wo tut es ihm weh? Make sentences!

My	head foot arm back leg tooth	hurts.

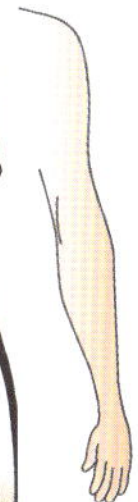

My head hurts.

____

____

____

____

____

Denke daran!

Es tut weh =
It hurts.
Die dritte Person Einzahl – er, sie, es – erkennt man am Ende des Verbs: am **(e)s**.

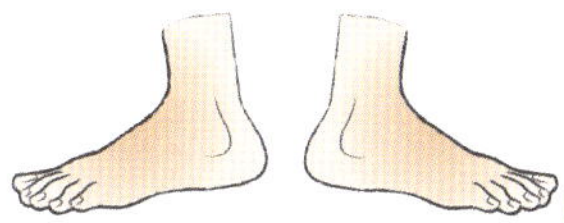

16. Aufgabe

Aber Captain Clever ist nicht nur verletzt, er ist auch noch krank. Weißt du, was er hat? Kennzeichne gleiche Aussagen mit gleichen Farben!

Ich habe eine Erkältung.

I am cold.

Ich bin krank.

What's the matter?

Ich habe Fieber.

Ich friere. / Mir ist kalt

I have a cold.

I have a temperature.

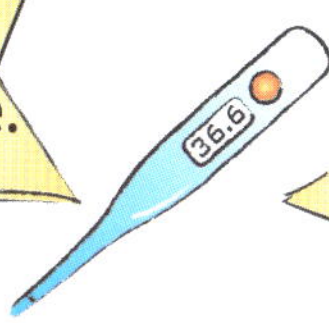

I am ill/sick.

17. Aufgabe

Hast du einen Rat für den kranken Captain Clever? Verbinde! Draw lines!

Get well soon!

Nimm Medizin!

Stay in bed!

Gute Besserung!

Bleib im Bett!

Take medicine!

Geh zum Doktor!

Go to the doctor's!

18. Aufgabe

Erinnere dich!
Im Englischen sagt man selten **I am** (ich bin), sondern man verbindet diese Wörter zu **I'm**.

Wenn Captain Clever auf seinen Reisen nach England kommt und jemanden trifft, begrüßt er ihn mit "How are you?" – „Wie geht es dir?". Draw lines!

19. Aufgabe

Schreibe deine eigenen Dialoge! Achte auf die Smileys. Nutze die Antworten aus Aufgabe 18. Write short dialogues!

How are you?
I'm fine, thanks and you?
I'm ok, thanks.

20. Aufgabe

Captain Clever schließt gern neue Freundschaften und übt Fragen, um mehr von jemandem zu erfahren. Übe mit ihm und verbinde die englischen und deutschen Sätze! Connect the English sentences and the German sentences with each other!

What's your name?	In welcher Klasse bist du?
Where are you from?	Bist du aus Deutschland?
How old are you?	Woher kommst du?
Are you from Germany?	Wie heißt du?
Which year are you in?	Wie alt bist du?

21. Aufgabe

Begrüße Captain Clever, frage nach seinem Namen, seinem Alter und woher er kommt!

Hello, what's your ______________?

Where ________ ______________?

How ________ ______________?

Which ________ ______________?

I am Captain Clever.
I am from Germany.
I am 10.
I am in the fourth year.

Erinnere dich!

What? = Was?
Where? = Wo? Woher?
Who? = Wer?
How? = Wie?

Tipp

Germany = Deutschland (Land)
German = Deutscher (Person)

Erinnere dich!

I am = ich bin
Im Englischen wird das **I** (ich) immer großgeschrieben.

Vergleichsbild

Im rechten Bild haben sich zwölf Fehler versteckt. Findest du sie?

4 am Faden

Gleich einem Faden reihen sich die vier Buchstaben des englischen Begriffs. Welcher Begriff ist es?

Der Begriff lautet:

____

22. Aufgabe

~~foot-~~ ~~chess~~ ~~cycl-~~ basket- base- table tennis

Captain Clever liebt Sport. Er und sein Papagei bestreiten viele Wettkämpfe. Finde heraus, in welchen Sportarten sie ihre Kräfte messen! From this list, write the full name in the correct column!

golf sail- climb- cricket ski- runn- volley- rid- tennis hand- surf- Formula 1 athletics darts fish-

-ball	-ing	other
football	cycling	chess

23. Aufgabe

Welches Sportgerät steht für welche Sportart? Write down your answers!

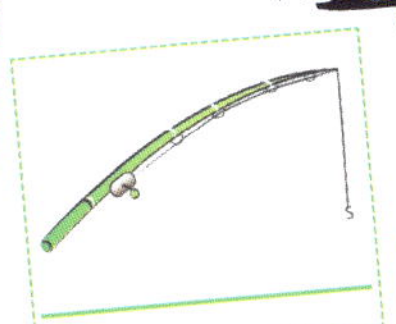

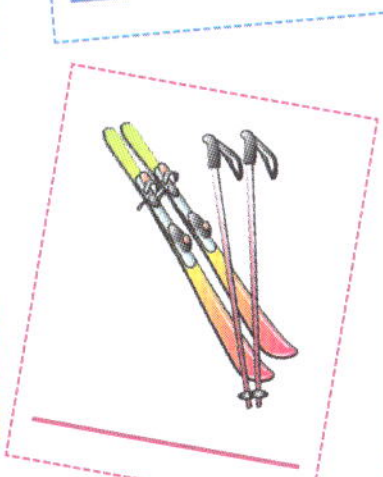

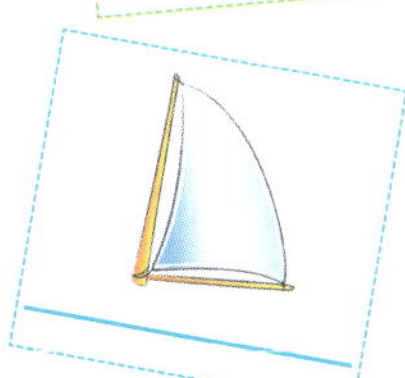

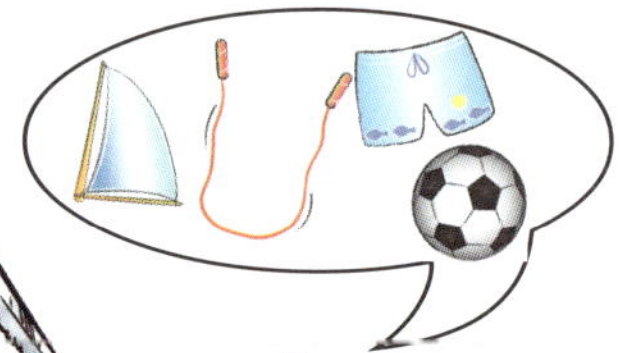

24. Aufgabe

Captain Clever, was sind deine Lieblingssportarten? What sports do you like?

I like surfing, rope-skipping, swimming and football.

Peter: I like cycling, ____________

____

____

Dave: ____________

____

____

____

Sue: ________________________

____

What sports do you like? Draw and write your favourite sports!

I like ________________________

____

Erinnere dich!

Wenn ich etwas mag, sage ich **I like**. Wenn ich wissen möchte, ob jemand etwas mag, frage ich **Do you like ...?** Wenn ich wissen will, was er mag, dann frage ich **What do you like?**

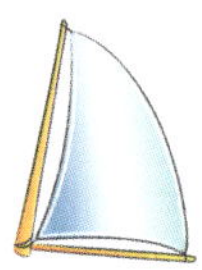

25. Aufgabe

Frage Captain Clever, welchen Sport er mag! Ask Captain Clever what sports he likes. Circle the correct answer!

Do you like football?	Yes, I do.	No, I don't.
Do you like basketball?	Yes, I do.	No, I don't.
Do you like swimming?	Yes, I do.	No, I don't.
Do you like riding?	Yes, I do.	No, I don't.
Do you like surfing?	Yes, I do.	No, I don't.

Erinnere dich!

Auf die Frage **Do you like ...?** (Magst du ...?) antwortest du mit **Yes, I do.** oder **No, I don't.**

26. Aufgabe

Captain Clever und seine Mannschaft sind den ganzen Tag auf den Beinen. Sie bewegen sich viel und haben dabei großen Spaß. Finde die Wörter, die zusammengehören, und schreibe sie auf!

Erinnere dich!

Don't = Do not
Du darfst etwas nicht machen!

27. Aufgabe

Auf Captain Clevers Insel gibt es auch Orte, wo etwas nicht erlaubt ist. Was darf man dort **nicht** machen? Draw lines!

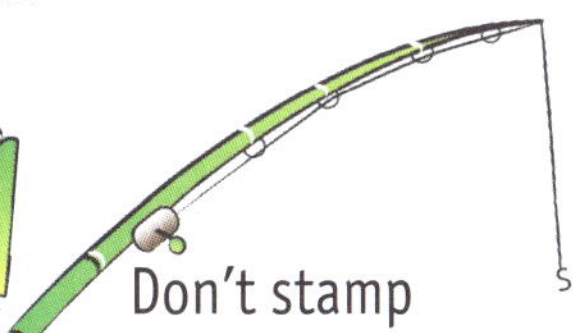

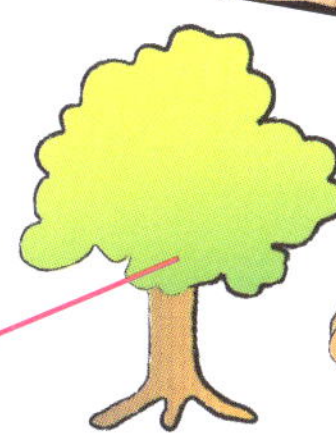

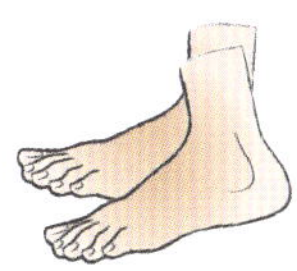

Don't stamp	trees.
Don't play	the cage.
Don't touch	off the bridge.
Don't jump	in the lake.
Don't go	with your feet.
Don't climb	fishing.
Don't open	football.
Don't swim	the wild animals.

28. Aufgabe

Denke daran!

once = 1x
twice = 2x
three times = 3x
four times = 4x
five times = 5x

Jetzt wird bald losgesegelt. Damit es auf dem Schiff nicht langweilig wird, haben Captain Clever und seine Freunde ein Spiel mit an Bord. Du kannst es auch spielen: Würfle und ziehe mit deinem Spielmännchen auf das entsprechende Feld. Wenn du auf ein Feld mit einer Aufforderung kommst, führe sie aus. Wie oft musst du würfeln, ehe du im Ziel ankommst? Viel Spaß!

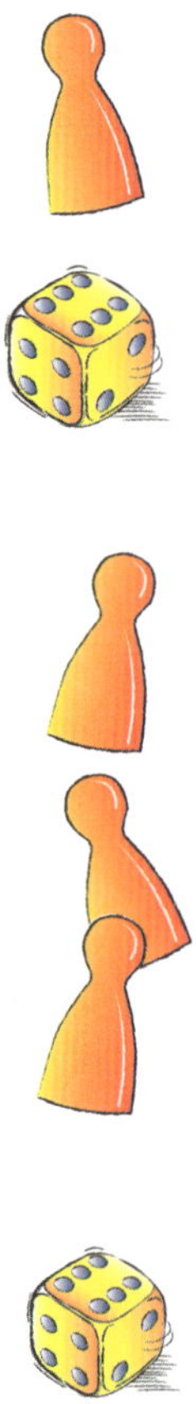

START 	1 Touch your left shoulder three times.	2 Clap your hands five times. 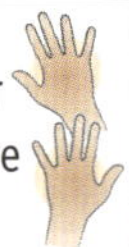	3	4 Shake your left hand.	5 Touch your mouth twice.
11 Bend your arms five times.	10 Close and open your eyes five times. 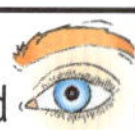	9 Touch your back.	8 Turn around three times. 	7 Go to a door.	6 
12 Touch your left knee four times.	23 Shake your left hand.	24 Miss a turn.	25 Sing a song. 	26 Touch your left foot seven times.	27 Open and close your mouth three times.
13 Shake your body.	22	21 Touch your nose.	20	19 Stamp your feet four times.	28
14 Bend your knees five times.	15 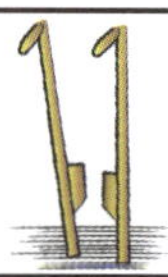	16 Jump up high five times.	17 	18 Be careful. Go back to number 10.	29 Climb onto a chair twice.
37 Stamp to the door.	36 Go around a table three times.	35 Touch your belly.	32	31 Shake your head.	30 Go to a window.
38 Shake your right hand.	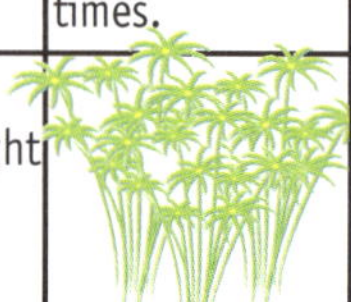	34 Miss a turn.	33 Bend your body four times.	44	45 Touch your right knee four times.
39	40 Touch your right foot four times.	41	42 Shake your right leg.	43	FINISH 

29. Aufgabe

Für die Reise müssen jede Menge Sachen eingepackt werden. Write the correct name under each picture!

nightie

boots	dress	rain jacket	blouse	
trainers	hat	sweater	gloves	
shorts	~~nightie~~	T-shirt	belt	
trousers	coat	skirt	swimming trunks	

30. Aufgabe

Diese Bekleidungsstücke hat Captain Clever in seinem Koffer. Stelle Fragen und beantworte sie!

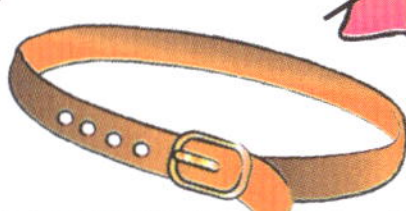
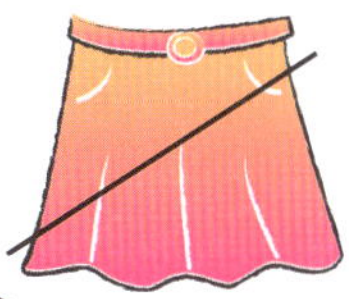

Is there a coat?
Is there ____________________
Is ____________________
____
____

Yes, there is.
______, ____________
______, ____________
No, ____________
______, ____________
______, ____________

Erinnere dich!
Antworte auf **Is there a ...?** entweder mit **Yes, there is** oder mit **No, there is not.**

Labyrinth

Nur ein Kind findet den Weg zu den Spielsachen. Welches ist es?

Was ist das?

Kannst du herausfinden, welcher Begriff hier dargestellt ist?

Lösung:

____

____

31. Aufgabe

Captain Clever probiert seine Sachen an. Schreibe auf, was er auszieht und dann anzieht! Write down, what he takes off and what he then puts on!

I take off my cap  and put on my hat .

I take off my ______________  and put on my ______________ .

I ______________  ______________ .

I ______________  ______________ 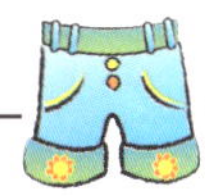.

I ______________  ______________ .

I ______________  ______________ .

Denke daran!

take off = Kleidung ausziehen
put on = Kleidung anziehen

32. Aufgabe

Klasse, alles passt! Jetzt verstaut Captain Clever alles in seiner Reisetruhe und schreibt auf, welche Dinge er besitzt. Leider sind ihm die Buchstaben dabei ziemlich durcheinandergeraten. Kannst du ihm helfen, sie wieder richtig zu sortieren? Be clever, Captain Clever.

Food and drink

3	8	15	3	15	12	1	19	5

33. Aufgabe

8	1	13

2	1	3	15	14

21	1	19	5	17

Seeleute putzen auf ihrer Reise ganz schön was weg. Finde heraus, was sie alles an Bord haben!

19	15	1	18	19

10	20	9	3	5

A	B	C	D	E	F	G	H	I	J	K	L	M	N	O	P	R	S	T	U	W	Y	Z
1	2	3	4	5	6	7	8	9	10	11	12	13	14	15	16	17	18	19	20	21	22	23

18	1	20	18	1	7	5

3	15	17	14	6	12	1	11	5	18

5	7	7

8	1	13	2	20	17	7	5	17

19	5	1

18	16	1	7	8	5	19	19	9

10	1	13

3	1	11	5

3	8	9	16	18

17	15	12	12

16	9	23	23	1

13	5	1	19

14	15	15	4	12	5	18

6	9	18	8

13	9	12	11

18	20	7	1	17

8	15	14	5	22

9	3	5	3	17	5	1	13

2	20	19	19	5	17

34. Aufgabe

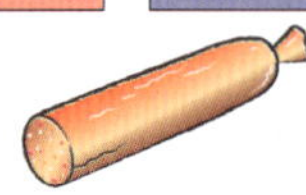

Was können Piraten trinken und essen? What do pirates drink and what do they eat? Please help!

water|meatbreadteacakejuicelemonadesausage

chipscheesecoffeebeerbuiscuitmilk

Denke daran!

Chips in Germany sind Crisps in Great Britain. Chips in Great Britain sind **Pommes** in Deutschland.

Pirates can drink	Pirates can eat
water	

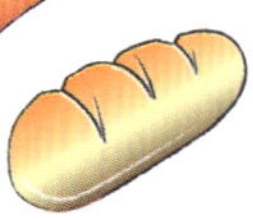

35. Aufgabe

pizza, eggs, cake, cucumber, toast, fish, potatoes, milk, tomatoes, chocolate, bread, juice, melons, honey, coffee, rolls, cheese, tea

Captain Clever, what do you like to eat and drink?
Streiche die Dinge durch, die er **nicht** mag!

Erinnere dich!

I like = ich mag
I don't like = ich mag nicht

36. Aufgabe

Und was magst du? And what do you like? Male und schreibe, was du gern isst und trinkst und was nicht!

I like ...

I don't like ...

Food and drink

37. Aufgabe

Denke daran!
he likes = er mag
she likes = sie mag
ABER:
he doesn't like = er mag nicht
she doesn't like = sie mag nicht

Lies den Text und du weißt, was andere Kinder gern essen. Read the text and you will know what other children like most to eat and drink. Male Smileys! Draw smileys!

likes ☺
doesn't like ☹

	sausages	chicken	cheese	juice	tea
Peter	☺				
Sue					
Sally					

Peter likes sausages and chicken, but he doesn't like cheese. He likes orange juice, but he doesn't like tea.

Sue loves animals and she doesn't like to eat sausage and chicken, she likes cheese and she likes juice and tea.

Sally likes all drinks and she likes chicken very much. She doesn't like sausage and cheese.

38. Aufgabe

Denke daran!
Mengen in Verpackungen werden immer mit **of** angegeben:
eine Büchse **mit** Bohnen = a tin **of** beans

Wieder diese verrückten Affen. Jemand hat vergessen, die Kombüse abzuschließen. Hilf aufräumen! Verbinde! Draw lines!

a carton of milk
a packet of tea
a jar of jam
a tin of beans
a basket of apples
a bar of chocolate
a bottle of wine

eine Büchse Bohnen
eine Flasche Wein
ein Korb Äpfel
ein Päckchen Tee
ein Karton Milch
ein Glas Marmelade
eine Tafel Schokolade

Schattenriss

Findest du heraus, welcher Schatten mit dem Frosch in der Mitte identisch ist?

Rebus

Finde zunächst heraus, welche Gegenstände hier dargestellt sind. Dann streiche die angegebenen Buchstaben und du findest die Lösung des Bilderrätsels!

Erinnere dich!

Beachte die Mehrzahlbildung:
pot – pots
ABER es gibt Ausnahmen:
knife – knives

39. Aufgabe

Captain Clever steht vor dem Geschirrschrank in seiner Kombüse. Hilf ihm, die Gegenstände richtig zu benennen!

Denke daran!

How ...? = Wie ...?
How many ...? = Wie viele ...?
How old ...? = Wie alt ...?

40. Aufgabe

Der letzte Sturm war heftig, einige Dinge sind zerbrochen. Wie viele Gegenstände sind kaputt? How many things are broken? Match the boxes!

les	6 pla	1 tea	5 cu
ps	pot	ses	4 bot
tles	3 bow	tes	2 glas

41. Aufgabe

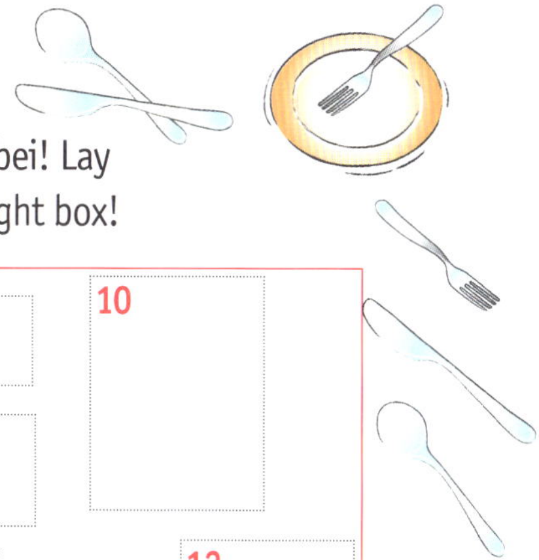

Nun muss Captain Clever den Tisch decken. Hilf ihm doch dabei! Lay the table! Zeichne die Dinge ein! Draw the things into the right box!

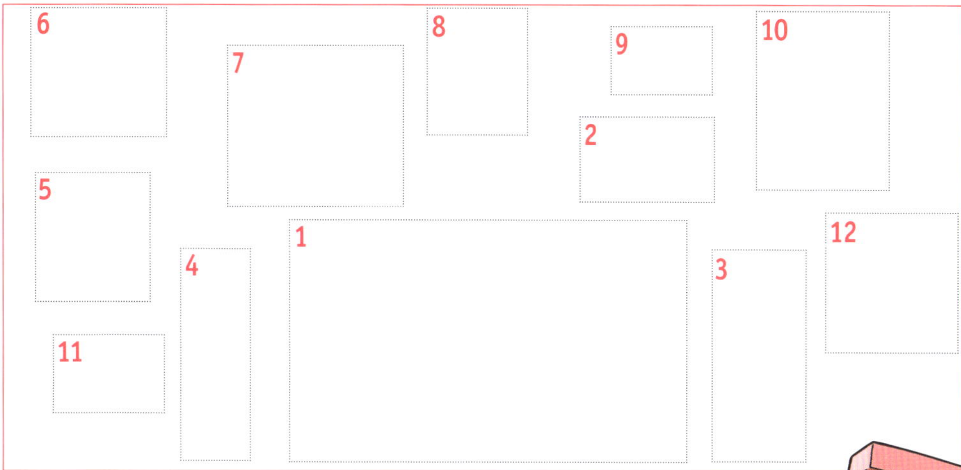

No.1 is a plate.
No. 2 is a cup and a saucer.
No. 3 is a knife and a spoon.
No. 4 is a fork.
No. 5 is a jar of jam.
No. 6 is a big bowl with cornflakes.
No. 7 are three rolls.
No. 8 is cheese.
No. 9 is sugar.
No. 10 is a carton of milk.
No. 11 is butter.
No. 12 is the teapot.

42. Aufgabe

Ein riesiger Topf steht auf dem Herd. Was hat der Koch dort alles hineingetan? Let's make a soup!

taem
tlas
snaeb
seotatop
storrac
reppep

Tipp

pepper =
1. Paprika
2. Pfeffer

43. Aufgabe

Nun hast du zusammen mit Captain Clever schon eine ganze Menge Englisch gelernt. Übe noch einmal die Zahlen und Farben! Find the numbers 2, 3, 4, 6, 7, 8, 9, 10, 11, 12, 13, 15, 20, 90, 50, 40, 60, 100 and the colours ! Search in all directions!

G	R	E	E	N	R	F	Y	T	R	O	F
K	E	L	U	U	B	E	O	D	M	R	I
C	D	T	E	Z	L	R	M	U	A	A	F
A	Z	H	I	L	Q	B	O	Q	R	N	T
L	N	T	O	R	E	R	W	W	B	G	Y
B	K	W	P	K	B	V	T	T	N	E	Y
S	V	E	F	I	F	T	E	E	N	D	T
S	E	L	G	Z	H	X	T	N	M	R	E
I	P	V	R	E	W	U	K	H	B	Z	N
X	L	E	E	A	Z	H	N	S	G	C	I
T	N	R	Y	N	A	R	I	D	D	I	N
Y	H	I	J	D	B	X	P	T	R	U	E
T	W	E	N	T	Y	T	H	R	E	E	J
Z	N	E	E	T	R	I	H	T	V	R	D

44. Aufgabe

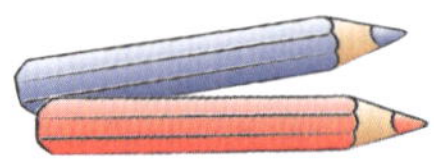

Übrigens, wenn du bis Hundert zählen kannst, dann kommst du auch bis Tausend! Probier es aus! Male die Wörter und Zahlen, die dasselbe bedeuten, in derselben Farbe an!

five hundred and ninety-one	452	three hundred and seventy-four	743	nine hundred and fifty-one
519	four hundred and twenty-five	195	four hundred and fifty-two	245
two hundred and forty-five	1000 one thousand	542	347	one hundred and ninety-five
seven hundred and forty-three	734	951	five hundred and nineteen	374
425	five hundred and forty-two	three hundred and forty-seven	591	seven hundred and thirty-four

45. Aufgabe

Bist du auch in den anderen gelernten Bereichen fit? Finde “the black sheep”. Ein Begriff gehört nicht in die Reihe. Finde ihn heraus und streiche ihn durch!

- eight new old quiet
- coat shoes cucumber belt
- brown black blue bag
- jump shake open tree
- swim surf sail comic
- fifty desk ruler rubber
- arm hand feet leg
- parrot pirat pupil child

Tipp
Prüfe Wortart, Oberbegriff und Mehrzahl!

46. Aufgabe

Oh dear, what’s that? Write every word in the right box!

feeling (6)

____

____

____

clothes (6)

____

____

____

food and drink (7)

____

____

____

activities (7)

____

____

____

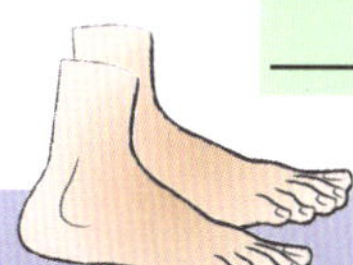

body (5)

____

____

____

Family and friends

47. Aufgabe

Captain Clever hat natürlich nicht nur seine Mannschaft, sondern auch eine große Familie. Weißt du, wer sie sind? Find out all persons of Captain Clever's family!

Kind ____________ Kinder ____________ Baby ____________

Vater ____________ Mutter ____________

Sohn ____________ Tochter ____________

Eltern ____________ Großeltern ____________

Großmutter ____________ Großvater ____________

Enkel ____________ Cousin ____________

Schwester ____________ Bruder ____________

Tante ____________ Onkel ____________

Freund ____________ Familie ____________

48. Aufgabe

Captain Clever ist auch mit vielen Tieren befreundet. Wer ist wo? Who is where? Beantworte die Fragen! Answer the questions!

Denke daran!

left = links
right = rechts
middle = Mitte
between = dazwischen

Who is in the middle? ____________

Who is on the left? ____________

Who is on the right? ____________

Who is on the right of Captain Clever? ____________

Who is on the left of the spider? ____________

Who is between the spider and the sheep? ____________

Who is between the mouse and the duck? ____________

After a time, the mouse goes to Captain Clever and is on the left of him. Who is in the middle now? ____________

49. Aufgabe

Wer ist wer? Who is who? A family tree.

grandchild · ~~brother~~ · father · uncle · sister · aunt · grandmother · son · grandfather · daughter · mother

Sally — Max grandfather
Bob — Elia grandmother

Lyn, Kate — Tom, George

Sue, Captain Clever, Peter

Peter is Captain Clever's brother.

Sue is Captain Clever's ______________.

Tom is his ______________.

Kate is his ______________.

Max is his ______________.

Elia is his ______________.

Captain Clever is Bob's ______________.

Tom is Bob's ______________.

George is Peter's ______________.

Lyn is Sue's ______________.

Kate is Sally's ______________.

Denke daran!

his brother = **sein** Bruder
her sister = **ihre** Schwester

50. Aufgabe

Use the right form: **am** or **are** or **is**!

I ______ Captain Clever. Peter ______ my brother and Sue ______ my sister. My parents ______ Kate and Tom. Lyn ______ my aunt and George ______ my uncle. Sally and Max ______ Kate's parents. She ______ my mother. Bob and Elia ______ Tom's parents. He ______ my father. Sally, Max, Elia and Bob ______ my grandparents.

Denke daran!

I am = ich bin
he is = er ist
she is = sie ist
they are = sie sind

Vergleichsbild

Im rechten Bild haben sich elf Fehler eingeschlichen. Wo stecken sie?

Umrissbild

Eines der kleinen Schafe stimmt der Form nach mit dem großen Schaf überein. Welches?

51. Aufgabe

Auch Captain Clever geht regelmäßig in die Schule. Was steht in seinem Klassenraum? What's in his classroom?

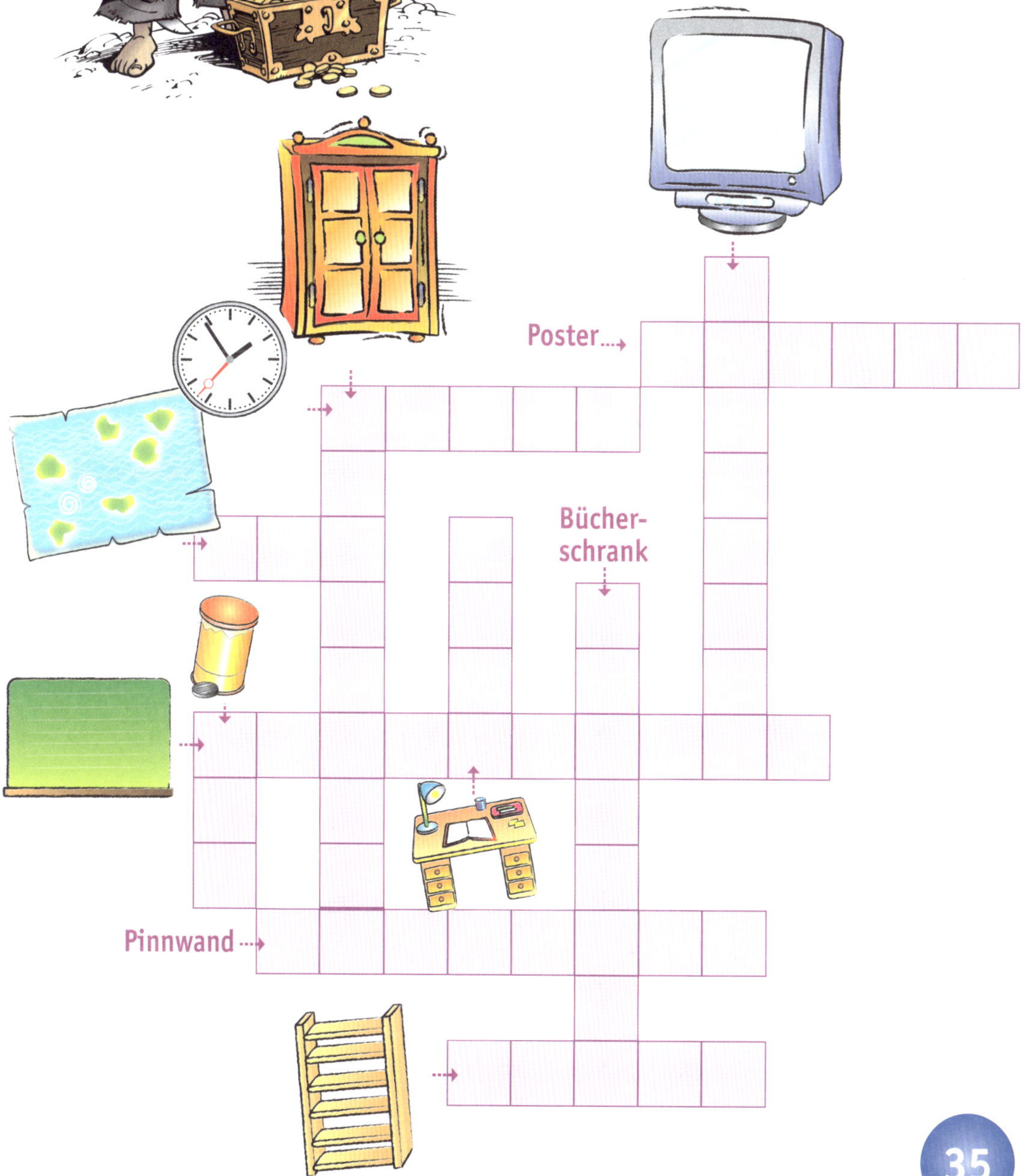

52. Aufgabe

How many things are in Captain Clever's school bag?

scissors marker scissors ~~pencil~~ ruler rubber
sharpener pen felt tip glue book marker
book ~~pencil~~ felt tip book ~~pencil~~ book
activity book rubber ruler marker felt tip
pencil case activity book book marker book

Erinnere dich!
How many? = Wie viele?

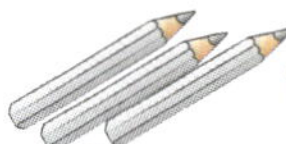 three pencils

 ____________________

 ____________________

 ____________________

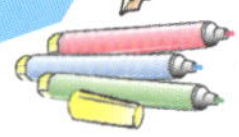 ____________________

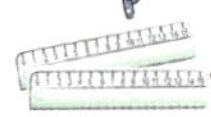 ____________________

 ____________________

 ____________________

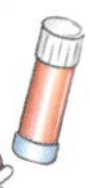 ____________________

 ____________________

 ____________________

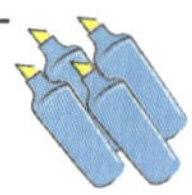 ____________________

53. Aufgabe

Auch Piraten haben den ganzen Tag in der Schule viel zu tun! Und was alles? Male die englische Übersetzung jeweils in der gleichen Farbe wie das deutsche Wort an!

		Listen to	Write		
	Write	Take	Look at	Take	
Speak	Read	Write	Read	Listen to	Speak
Read	Write	Listen to	Take	Look at	Write
Listen to	Look at	Write	Speak	Speak	Read
	Take	Look at	Write	Take	
		Read	Listen to		

54. Aufgabe

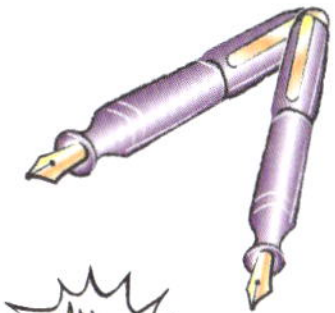

Nun hast du schon wieder eine ganze Menge gelernt. Hier kannst du noch einmal manches davon üben. Welche Gegenstände nimmst du, um gemeinsam was zu machen? Let's do something together!

scissors
~~songtext~~
pencil
book
paint box
pen

read a story.
paint a giraffe.
~~sing a song.~~
draw a circle.
write a letter.
cut out flowers.

Take your songtext.
Take your ____________

____
____
____
____

Let's sing a song.
Let's ____________

____
____
____
____

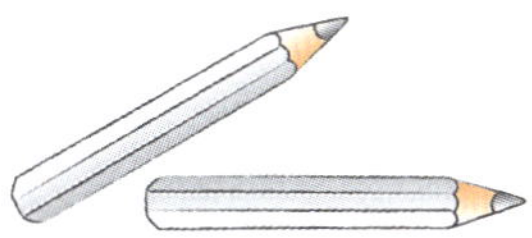

Tipp

Wenn du jemanden aufforderst, beginnst du wie im Deutschen mit dem Verb:
Nimm ... = **Take ...**
Lass uns ... = **Let's ...**

55. Aufgabe

Folge den Schritten! Immer wenn ein C (für colour) steht, dann male das Kästchen aus!

S – left C left C down C three to the left C up C left C down C two to the left C up C left C two to the left C down C one down one to the right C right C three to the right C two to the right C two to the right C right C right C three to the right C up C right C right C down C three to the right C up C up C up C up C right C two to the left C three to the left C four to the left C left C left C two to the left C left C left C two to the left C left C left C one to the left one down C five to the right C two to the right C two to the right C five to the right C two to the right C down C two to the left C

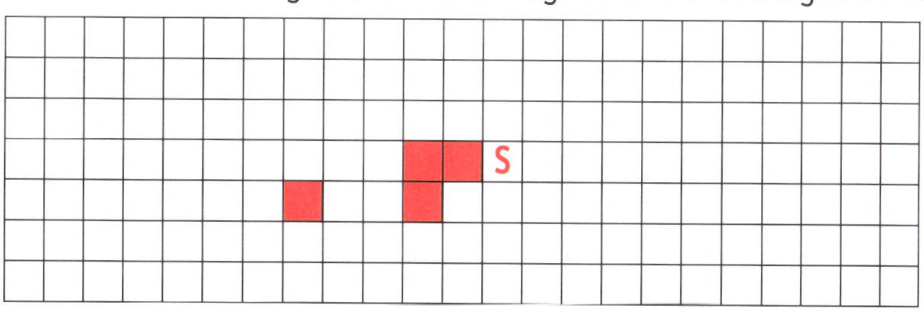

Tipp

Es ist höflich, wenn du bei Fragen mit **Excuse me** (Entschuldigung) beginnst.

56. Aufgabe

Auch ein Pirat kann mal was vergessen. Frage, ob du etwas haben kannst! Put up questions!

have pencil, your please? ~~I~~ ~~Can~~

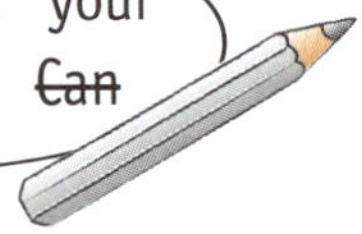

Can I ______________________

____

your me rubber, Give please.

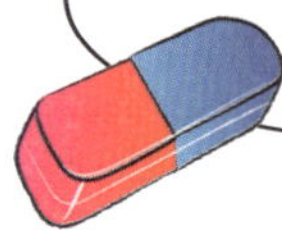

____

____

have your please? I Can glue,

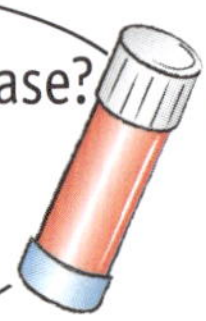

____

____

your sharpener, me Give please.

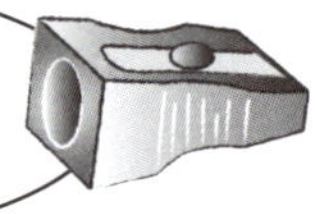

____

____

have scissors, your please? I Can

____

____

Thank you. / Here you are.

57. Aufgabe

Captain Clever muss für die Reise viel Holz zum Heizen vorbereiten und dafür Baumstämme zersägen. Hilf ihm und finde jeweils die gegenteilige Bedeutung!

big long cold sad bad ~~right~~ old down day

left – right

short – ______

young – ______

little – ______

up – ______

night – ______

hot – ______

happy – ______

good – ______

58. Aufgabe

Ein Piratenjahr hat die gleichen Monate wie unser Jahr. Captain Clevers Kalender hat im Laufe der Seereisen allerdings einige Wasserspritzer abbekommen. Fill in the right letters!

a a a a a
a a e e e e
e e e e e e
e i o o o u
u u u u

J nu ry — F br ry
M rch — pr l — M y
J n — J ly — g st
S pt mb r — ct b r
N v mb r — D c mb r

59. Aufgabe

Im Kalender stehen auch die "days of the week": die Wochentage. Aber irgendwie hat der Papagei immer wieder seinen Lieblingsbuchstaben reingeschmuggelt. Streiche alle P weg und schreibe die Wochentage noch einmal richtig auf!

MOPNPDAPY ____________________
PTUEPSPDPAY ____________________
WEDPPNEPSDPAY ____________________
PTHPPURPSDAPY ____________________
FPPRPIDPAY ____________________
PSATUPRPDAYP ____________________
SPUPNPDPPAY ____________________

Captain Clever's week

60. Aufgabe

Denke daran!
which = welche, welcher, welches

Captain Clevers Papagei plappert los: "Today is Thursday, tomorrow is Friday and yesterday was Wednesday." Is it right? Captain Clever sieht in sein Logbuch. Darin steht:

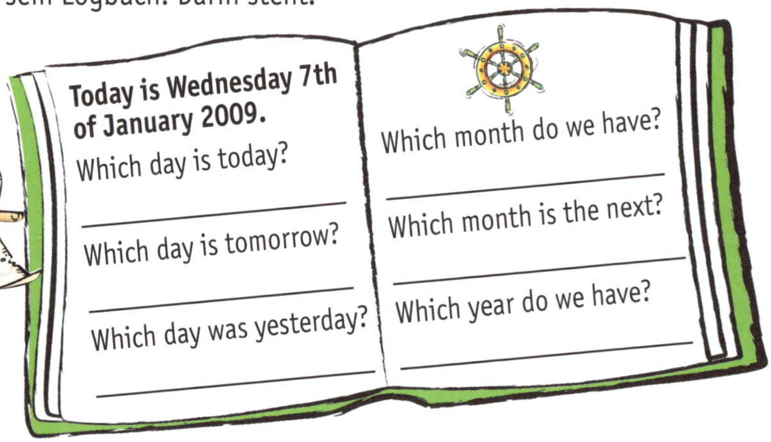

61. Aufgabe

Erinnere dich!
Im Englischen gibt es ein Zwölf-Stunden-System. Um Vormittag und Nachmittag zu unterscheiden, verwendet man **a. m.** = vormittags und **p. m.** = nachmittags.
It's one o'clock a. m./
It's one o'clock p. m.

What's the time? Nein, keine Sorge, du musst dich nicht nach den Sternen richten, lies einfach die Zeiten auf den Uhren ab oder trage die Zeiger ein!

Ausmalbild

Dieses Bild kannst du ausmalen, wie es dir gefällt!

Gleiche suchen

Zwei Dudelsackspieler sind farblich und der Form nach identisch. Findest du heraus, welche es sind?

62. Aufgabe

Male gleiche Zeiten mit gleicher Farbe aus! Paint the same times with the same colour!

Tipp

half past six =
„halb nach sechs"
= halb sieben

63. Aufgabe

Oh, dieser neugierige Papagei. Er hat im Logbuch des Kapitäns gelesen. Stimmt das, was der Papagei über Captain Clevers Tagesablauf erzählt? Put it in the right order!

- ❑ I have breakfast at seven o'clock.
- ❑ I do my homework at four o'clock.
- ❑ I get up at six o'clock.
- ❑ I go to bed at nine o'clock.
- ❑ I wash my face and dress at half past six.
- ❑ I go to my pirate school at eight o'clock.
- ❑ I have lunch at seven o'clock in the evening.
- ❑ I go home at two o'clock in the afternoon.
- ❑ At five o'clock I play games and feed the animals.

64. Aufgabe

Captain Clever hat auf seiner Insel vielen Tieren ein Zuhause gegeben.
There are many animals on Captain Clever's island. Name the animals!

	lion tiger monkey		bear bee seal		fish zebra shark
	lion fox guinea pig		budgie camel pony		turkey frog elephant
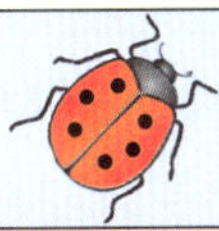	ladybird butterfly bee		hippo whale dolphin		rabbit penguin whale
	giraffe crocodile owl		budgie ladybird blackbird		monkey owl guinea pig

65. Aufgabe

Noch mehr Tiere. Trage sie ein und du erhältst ein Lösungswort!

66. Aufgabe

Captain Clever zeigt uns seine Tiere. Sage, was du von Nahem und was du von Weitem für Tiere siehst. Sprich so: **This** is a ... and **that** is a ...

lion giraffe turtle bear elephant bat rhino rabbit snail horse sheep mouse

This is a ______________________________

and that is a ______________________________

Denke daran!
This is ... steht für nahe dran.
That is ... steht für etwas weiter weg.

67. Aufgabe

Put down **is** or **are**!

1. There _______ birds in the nest.
2. There _______ a zebra in the grass.
3. There _______ monkeys in the trees.
4. There _______ a cow on the river.
5. There _______ fish in the sea.
6. There _______ rabbits in the cage.
7. There _______ budgies in the birdcage.
8. There _______ some flowers on the meadow.
9. There _______ a caterpillar on the leaf.
10. There _______ three lions in three cages.

68. Aufgabe

So viele Tiere und einige haben wir noch gar nicht gesehen. Lasst uns Captain Clever fragen, welche Tiere noch auf seiner Insel leben!

Have you got

crocodiles?	Yes, I have.
rhinos?	Yes, ______________.
monkeys?	Yes, ______________.
a giraffe?	Yes, ______________.
horses?	Yes, ______________.
a snake?	Yes, ______________.
a polar bear?	No, ______________.
a whale?	No, ______________.

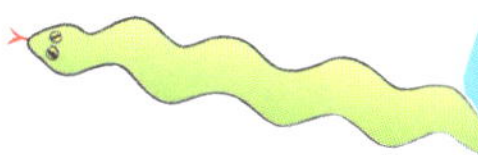

Denke daran!

Wenn du wissen möchtest, ob jemand etwas hat oder besitzt, dann fragst du: **Have you got ...?** (Hast du ...?). Antworte mit **Yes, I have** oder **No, I haven't.**

Erinnere dich!

haven't = have not

69. Aufgabe

Auf der Insel gibt es außerdem Seen, Bäume, Flüsse, Blumen und einen Dschungel. Um die Insel herum ist das Meer. Trage in die leeren Kästchen die noch fehlenden Wörter ein! Und zwar so, dass in jeder Reihe, jeder Spalte und in jedem dick umrahmten Kästchen jeder der Begriffe nur einmal vorkommt!

		lakes	sea	trees	
jungle		sea		flowers	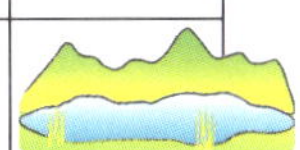
			jungle		
lakes	sea				rivers
	flowers	jungle	trees		

Denke daran!

lake = See
sea = Meer

Denke daran!

can (können) steht immer mit einem Verb zusammen.

70. Aufgabe

Was Tiere können. What animals are able to do. Here is something wrong. Correct the sentences!

Budgies can catch mice.
Cats can fly.

____

____

Tigers can jump.
Kangaroos can run.

____

____

Fish can climb trees.
Monkeys can swim.

____

____

Snakes can shake their body.
Lions can creep.

____

____

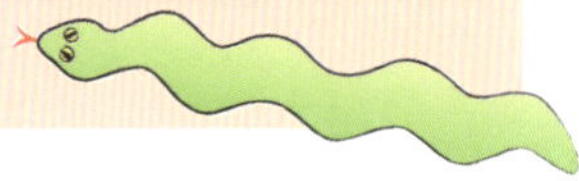

71. Aufgabe

Captain Clever has got three lions. Finde heraus, wie sie heißen, in welchem Käfig sie sitzen, wie alt sie sind, woher sie kommen und was sie am liebsten machen!

cage			
name			
how old			
is from			
likes			

1. One lion likes sleeping.
2. One lion comes from Tansania.
3. The lion who likes catching balls comes from South Africa.
4. King is twelve years old.
5. Robin isn't seven years old.
6. Robin isn't from Kenia.
7. John lives between King and Robin.
8. John likes catching balls.
9. One lion is nine years old.
10. Robin likes swimming.
11. One lion is seven years old.
12. King is in the left cage.

Erinnere dich!

Namen von Personen, Tieren, Ländern, Nationalitäten sowie Monate, bestimmte Gebäude und Festtage werden großgeschrieben.

72. Aufgabe

Auch an Captain Clever gehen die Jahreszeiten nicht spurlos vorüber. Was ist typisch für die Jahreszeiten? What's typical for the seasons?

winter spring autumn summer snow rain wet
dry cold icy sunbathing swimming Easter
snowman kite snowdrop Halloween Christmas
beach sun ice cream holidays falling leaves tulip

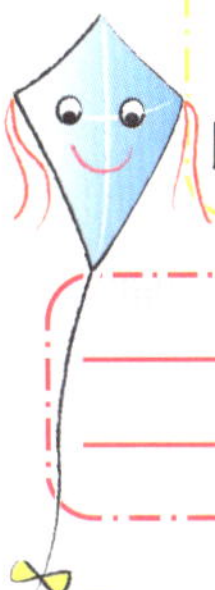

73. Aufgabe

Hier sind einige Begriffe aus Captain Clevers Logbuch. Weißt du, was sie bedeuten? Verbinde! Here are some words from Captain Clever's logbook. Do you know what they mean? Connect them!

 rainbow	warm or cold
temperature	
thunderstorm	the light and heat of the sun
lightning	what will happen next
calendar	a storm with strong winds 
forecast	
 sunshine	 a very short light in the sky
hurricane	a storm with lightning  
umbrella	days, months and years

74. Aufgabe

What a crazy weather! Was für ein verrücktes Wetter! Captain Clevers Papagei fliegt über die Insel und gerät in ständig anderes Wetter. Wohin fliegt der Papagei? Where does the bird fly?

75. Aufgabe

In Captain Clevers Logbuch stehen für vier Tage folgende Wetteraufzeichnungen. Übertrage die Informationen mithilfe von Symbolen in die Tabelle! Put down the symbols on the table!

Monday: The sun is shining and it is very warm.
Tuesday: The weather is crazy; sometimes it is sunny, sometimes it is windy and sometimes it is raining.
Wednesday: It is very cloudy and cold.
Thursday: It is very sunny and there are only a few clouds in the sky.

Mo______	Tu______	Wed________	Th_____
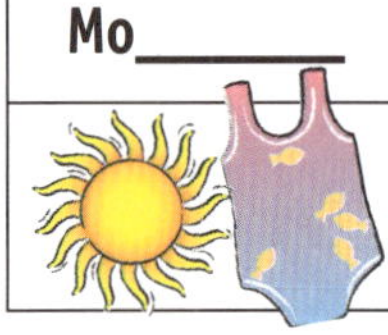			

Was ist das?

Kannst du herausfinden, welcher Begriff hier dargestellt ist?

Lösung: ______________
____

Labyrinth

Nur ein Kind findet den Weg zum See. Welches Kind kann schwimmen gehen?

peaches, box, tooth, mouse, sheep

76. Aufgabe

Erinnere dich!

Einige unregelmäßige Mehrzahlformen unterscheiden sich vollständig von der Einzahlform, manche nur teilweise und manche gar nicht.

Captain Clever hat mit dem Englischen manchmal seine Probleme. Manchmal erkennt er die Mehrzahl nicht sofort. Verbinde Einzahl und Mehrzahl miteinander und kennzeichne die Einzahl mit einer Farbe und die Mehrzahl mit einer anderen! Connect and mark plural and singular forms!

child, shelves, sheep, knife, leaves, women, teeth, mice, peach, fish, shelf, fish, feet, leaf, knives, boxes, woman, foot, children

Denke daran!

Endet ein Wort mit einem Zischlaut (s; ss; sh; ch; x) wird am Ende **-es** geschrieben. Dann spricht man -is. [boksis]

77. Aufgabe

Außerdem hat Captain Clever manchmal Probleme mit dem Wortschatz. Um zu üben, hat er ein lustiges Spiel erfunden: Pro Fisch gehören immer zwei Wörter zu dem fetten Wort. Finde sie heraus! Always two words belong to the first!

- **month**: rainy, May, April, clouds, tigers
- **nature**: summer, tree, spider, ruler, aunt
- **school**: ice cream, clouds, rubber, autumn, desk
- **weather**: snake, rainbow, foggy, spring, book
- **family**: sister, hamster, grandmother, star, icy
- **nature**: number, rose, daffodil, bag, yellow
- **school**: write, uncle, rain, moon, listen to
- **season**: week, autumn, spring, poster, map
- **time**: big, watch, child, letter, clock
- **animals**: bat, boy, today, seal, tulip

78. Aufgabe

Captain Clever kennt noch weitere Spiele, um den englischen Wortschatz zu üben: Complete the pictures!

 a tree on the island	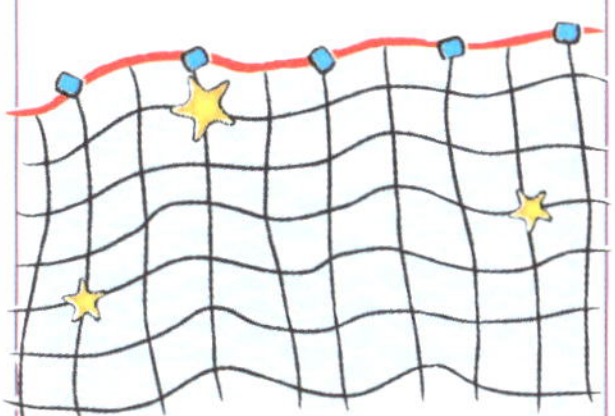 three fish in the net	 a bird on the hat
 mice behind the cupboard	 flowers between the trees	 a snake under the chair
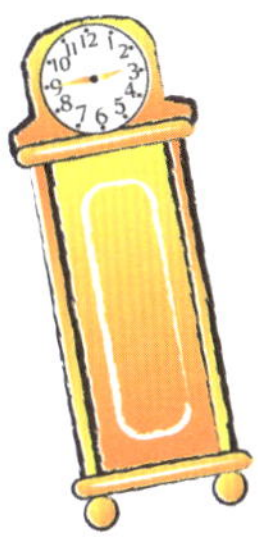 a ghost next to the clock	 an elephant opposite the mouse	 a snowman behind the letter box
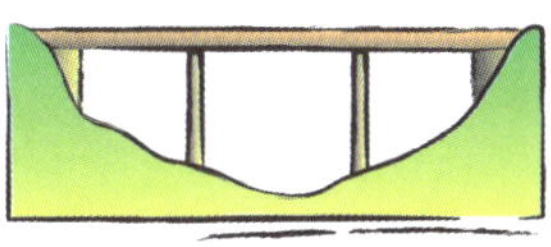 a rainbow over the bridge	 a pumpkin next to the straw man	 the sun over the ship

79. Aufgabe

Hilf Captain Clever beim Luftballon-Sortieren:
Do you know the right word? Connect the balloons!

darüber

in

dahinter

over

next to

daneben

on

darin

behind

gegen-über

opposite

darauf

80. Aufgabe

Nun möchte Captain Clever es aber allen zeigen, wie gespenstisch viele englische Wörter er kennt! Kannst du das auch? Beachte die Groß- und Kleinschreibung!

a is for ______________________

c is for ______________________

e is for ______________________

g is for ______________________

i is for ______________________

l is for ______________________

n is for ______________________

p is for ______________________

r is for ______________________

s is for ______________________

t is for ______________________

u is for ______________________

v is for ______________________

w is for ______________________

y is for ______________________

z is for ______________________

b is for ______________________

d is for ______________________

f is for ______________________

h is for ______________________

k is for ______________________

m is for ______________________

o is for ______________________

q is for ______________________

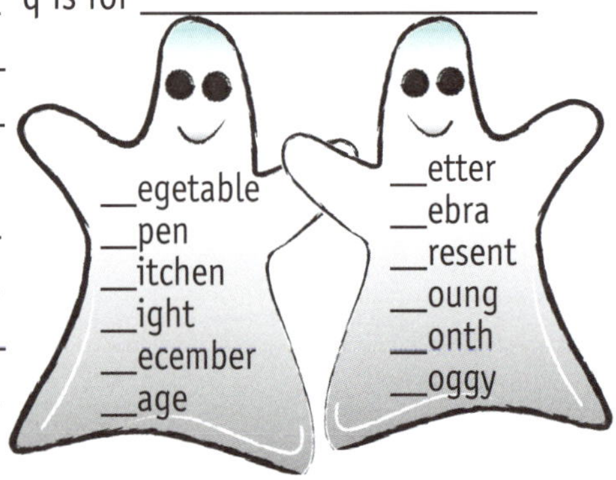

81. Aufgabe

Captain Clever feiert im Laufe des Jahres viele verschiedene Feste. Vervollständige die Wörter und verbinde sie mit dem dazugehörigen Bild! Finish the words and match with one picture!

> **Denke daran!**
> Feiertage, die als Eigenname stehen, werden großgeschrieben.

East______

birth______

______ Year

Valentine's ______

______llowee___

Thanks______ing

______mas

82. Aufgabe

Captain Clever möchte seinen Verwandten zu allen Festtagen Postkarten schreiben. Was soll er schreiben, ...

... wenn jemand Geburtstag hat? ______________________

... wenn Ostern ist? ______________________

... wenn Weihnachten gefeiert wird? ______________________

... wenn ein neues Jahr beginnt? ______________________

... wenn jemand in die Ferien fährt? ______________________

... wenn Erntedankfest gefeiert wird? ______________________

... wenn Halloween ist? ______________________

... wenn Valentinstag ist? ______________________

Happy Valentine.

Happy Thanksgiving.

Happy Easter.

Trick or treat.

Have nice holidays.

Happy New Year.

Happy birthday.

Merry Christmas.

Denke daran!

Monate werden großgeschrieben.

83. Aufgabe

Captain Clever hat sich mal wieder ein Spiel für dich ausgedacht: Welche Maus frisst welches Stückchen Käse? Draw lines!

84. Aufgabe

Und noch ein Rätsel: Welcher Monat wird beschrieben? Which month is described?

Valentine's day is in ______________________________.

This month we celebrate Christmas is ______________________.

Easter is in ______________________ or ____________________.

People wish "Happy New Year" in ____________________________.

When do you have your big holidays? My big holidays are in

____________________________________.

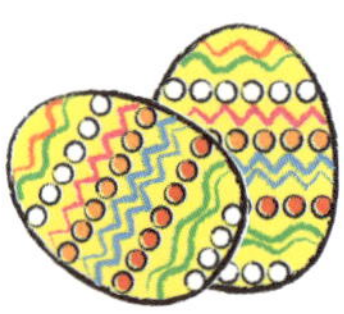

And when is your birthday? My birthday is in __________________.

Halloween is in the night from 31. ____________________

to 1. ________________________.

85. Aufgabe

Wenn er groß ist, möchte Captain Clever auch gern mal in einem Haus mit vielen Möbeln wohnen. Vervollständige! Complete the drawings!

chair	bed	table	door
cupboard	window	fridge	picture
lamp	television	stairs	sofa

Tipp
castle = Schloss
house = Haus

86. Aufgabe

Kennst du den Spruch "My home is my castle"? Typisch British ...
Nein, kein castle (Schloss), nur ein Haus (house) möchte Captain Clever. Welche Zimmer und Teile eines Hauses erkennst du?
Which rooms and parts of a house do you recognise?

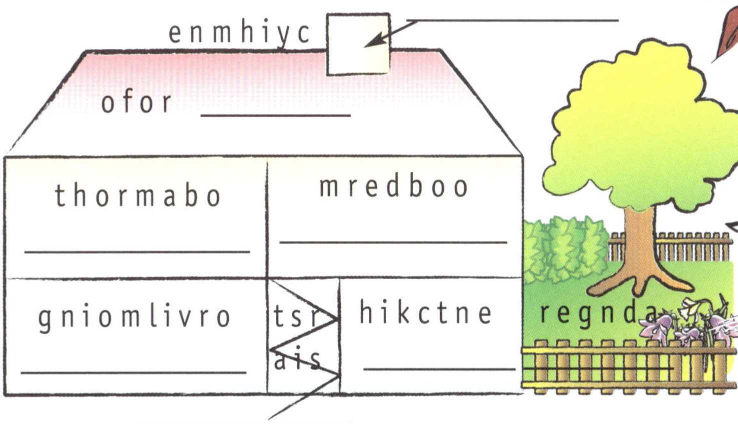

Vergleichsbild

Im rechten Bild haben sich zehn Fehler versteckt. Findest du sie?

Englisches Rebus

Finde zunächst heraus, welche Gegenstände hier dargestellt sind und schreibe jeweils die englische Übersetzung auf. Dann streiche die angegebenen Buchstaben oder füge sie hinzu und du findest die Lösung des Bilderrätsels!

87. Aufgabe

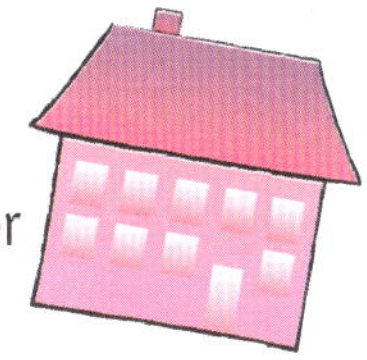

Gehe in die Küche, ins Wohnzimmer, in das Schlafzimmer und in dein Zimmer. What have you got there?

Tipp

galley = kitchen on a ship = Kombüse

kitchen

____

____

____

____

living room

sofa, ______________________

____

____

____

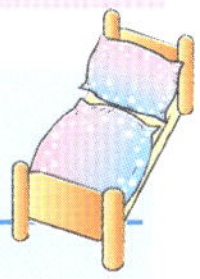

bedroom

____

____

____

____

my room

desk, ______________________

____

____

____

88. Aufgabe

Überall Mäuse in der Kombüse! Zeige Captain Clever, wo sie sind, indem du sie einzeichnest. There are mice everywhere in the galley. Mark them!

There is one mouse on one chair.
There is one mouse on the cupboard.
There are two mice under the table.
There are two mice in the basket.
There is one mouse between the two cups.
There is one mouse in the fridge.
There are two mice behind the cupboard.
There is a mouse in one cup.
There are three mice under the cupboard.

How many mice are in the kitchen? ______________

89. Aufgabe

flower · grocery · store · office · market · shop · agent · ery

Wenn Captain Clever an Land ist, geht er einkaufen. Wo kauft er ein? These are the most important shops for Captain Clever.
Vervollständige! Complete!

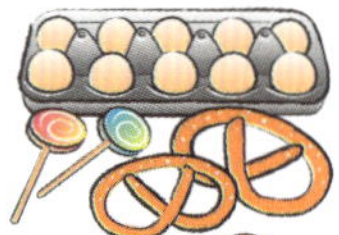

Bäcker (place)	bak___________
Supermarkt	super___________
Post	post___________
Spielwarenladen	toy___________
Zeitungshändler	news___________
Warenhaus	department___________
Blumenladen	___________shop
Obst- und Gemüseladen	green___________

90. Aufgabe

Was kann er dort jeweils kaufen? What can he buy there?
The first one is done for you.

dolls rolls stamps	post office stamps	bakery ___________	toy shop ___________
roses oranges newspapers	flower shop ___________	newsagent ___________	supermarket ___________
bottles of milk model car trousers	department store ___________	supermarket ___________	toy shop ___________
comics potatoes cakes	newsagent ___________	bakery ___________	greengrocery ___________
grapes jar of jam card games	toy shop ___________	greengrocery ___________	supermarket ___________

Denke daran!
shop = **store** =
Laden, Geschäft

91. Aufgabe

Hier ist Captain Clevers Einkaufsliste. Here is Captain Clever's shopping list.

a box of e____________
a kilo of t____________
a pound of b____________
a bottle of m____________
a box of c____________
a bottle of o ____________
one pound of m____________
a bar of c____________

-hocolate
-range juice
-omatoes
-eat
-ornflakes
-ilk
-ggs
-utter

Erinnere dich!

pound hat mehrere Bedeutungen:
a) Geld: one pound = 1£ = 100 pence (1 penny)
b) Gewicht: 454g = one pound

92. Aufgabe

Wo kauft Captain Clever, wo bezahlt er und wo wird ihm etwas verkauft? Setze ein: **buy** (kaufen) – **pay** (bezahlen) – **sell** (verkaufen)!

At the baker's I __________ (kaufe) bread.

I _______________ (kaufe) comics at the newsagent's.

In the post office I ____________ (bezahle) the stamps.

In the flower shop I ____________ (kaufe) roses.

Department stores ______________ (verkaufen) trousers and shoes.

In the toy shop I __________ (bezahle) with money.

Greengrocers ____________ (verkaufen) apples and cucumbers.

93. Aufgabe

Denke daran!
Es gibt zwei Möglichkeiten Geldbeträge zu sagen:
£ 2.75 =
1. two pound seventy-five
2. two seventy-five

Na das hat sich ja gelohnt, Captain Clever! Was hat er heute bezahlt? What has he paid today?

supermarket

butter	£	1,15
2 bottles of milk	£	____
sausages	£	7,75
Total	£	10,90

restaurant

a cup of tea	£	1,90
2 glasses of water	£	____
3 pieces of cake	£	5,85
Total	£	10,95

bakery

6 rolls	£	2,50
bread	£	3,25
lemon cake	£	10,50
Total	£	____

toy shop

racing car	£	7,35
teddy bear	£	11,85
helicopter	£	9,75
puzzle	£	4,20
Total	£	____

94. Aufgabe

Tipp
has paid kommt von pay (bezahlen) und ist die Vergangenheitsform = hat bezahlt.

Wenn du Captain Clevers Kassenzettel aus Aufgabe 93 ansiehst, weißt du, wie viel auf seiner Insel die jeweiligen Sachen kosten!

How much is a packet of butter? ____________________

How much is a helicopter? ____________________

How much is a bread? ____________________

How much are two glasses of water? ____________________

How much are the two bottles of milk? ____________________

How much are six rolls? ____________________

How much Captain Clever has paid at the baker's? ____________________

How much are the toys? ____________________

95. Aufgabe

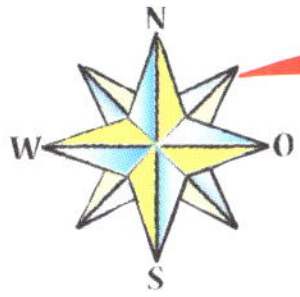

Auf der Pirateninsel gibt es viele Orte zum Besuchen, Mitmachen und Bestaunen. Trage die Himmelsrichtungen in die Karte ein und zeichne alle anderen Plätze an ihre richtige Stelle!
Put down North – South – East – West!

Denke daran!
Norden = **north**
Nordpol = **the North Pole**
im Norden = **in the north**
in den Norden = **to the north**

In the north there is a soccer pitch (It is a place where children play football).
In the south there is a playground and a sports field.
In the east there are two parks, one for wild animals and a children's zoo.
In the west there is a beach and an adventure playground.

96. Aufgabe

Was kann Captain Clever wo machen?
What can he do there? Put down yes!

What can Captain Clever do there?	play-ground	soccer pitch	children's zoo	sports field	beach
play tennis				yes	
go swimming					
play football					
ride ponies					
feed the animals					
go climbing					
play ball					
go sailing					
make sand castles					

97. Aufgabe

An welchem Ort sind die Kinder? At which place are the children?

Kate: I can't play football. I like tennis. sports field

Steven: I am a very good football player. ____________________

Captain Clever: My hobby is climbing. ____________________

Anne: I like swimming. ____________________

Peter: I like watching animals. ____________________

Tom: I would like to stroke animals. ____________________

Sue: I would like to see a tiger. ____________________

98. Aufgabe

Hi Captain Clever, wie komme ich zum Abenteuerspielplatz? How can I get to the adventure playground? "First you sail over the sea, climb over the mountains, jump over the river, go through the wood, then swim across the lake, go along the beach, go over the bridge and finally ride to the adventure playground."

Here I am.

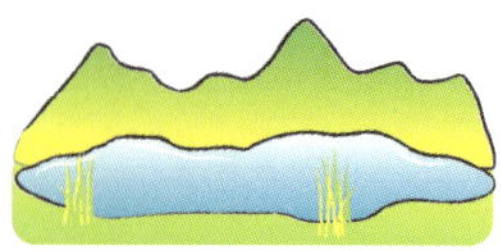

Denke daran!

Beachte die Position von **like**:
I like = ich mag (von mögen)
I would like to ... = ich würde gern (etw. machen)
it looks like ... = es sieht aus wie ...

Schattenriss

Welcher Schatten ist mit dem farbigen Huhn identisch?

Punktebild

Verbinde die Punkte den einzelnen Zahlen nach und du wirst ein Tier erkennen!

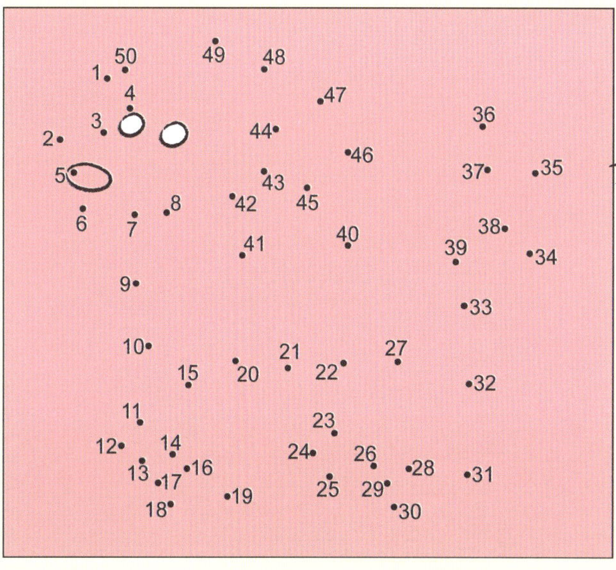

Enjoy travelling

99. Aufgabe

Denke daran!
Wenn du ausdrückst, mit welchem Verkehrsmittel du fährst, verwendest du immer **to go by:** to go by bus, to go by train

Captain Clever reist stets mit seinem Schiff um die Welt. Welche Transportmittel kennst du noch? Paint the same things with the same colour!

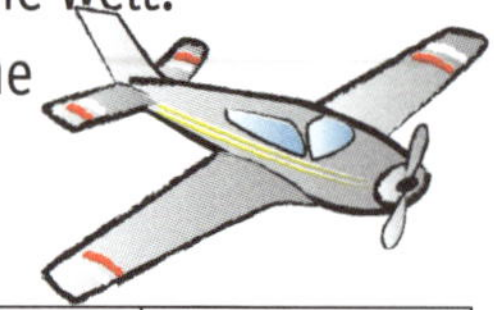

spaceship	bus	Rennauto	sailing boat	LKW
Motorrad	bike	helicopter	U-Bahn	racing car
tractor	motorbike	lorry	Flugzeug	Traktor
Segelboot	rocket	train	Raumschiff	Fahrrad
Bus	Hubschrauber	plane	Underground	Zug

Ein Fahrzeug steht allein, welches und was ist es?

____________________________ = ___________________________

100. Aufgabe

Wie möchtest du wohin reisen? How would you like to travel there?

I'd like to go to Great Britain by ______________________________.

I'd like to go to Australia by ______________________________.

I'd like to go to Berlin by ______________________________.

I'd like to go to the USA by ______________________________.

And now you:

I'd like to go to ____________________ by ____________________.

I'd like to go to ____________________ by ____________________.

I'd like to go to ____________________ by ____________________.

Tipp
I'd like = **I would like** = Ich würde gern

101. Aufgabe

Captain Clever kennt sich nur mit Schiffen gut aus. Bei den anderen Fahrzeugen braucht er Hilfe. Welches Fahrzeug stoppt wo?
Which vehicle stops where?

102. Aufgabe

Where is the next underground? Wo ist der nächste U-Bahnhof?

Where is the next ______________________ (Bushaltestelle)?

Where is the next ______________________ (Bahnhof)?

Where is the next ______________________ (Flughafen)?

Where is the next ______________________ (Taxi Halt)?

Tipp

Die U-Bahn in London heißt **The Tube.**

103. Aufgabe

Wenn du reist, Captain Clever, dann stecke immer das richtige Geld ein! If you travel, Captain Clever, always take the right money! Draw lines!

104. Aufgabe

Tipp
bigger = größer
capital = Hauptstadt

Kennst du die Abkürzung GB? Und weißt du auch, was sie bedeutet? GB = Great Britain = Großbritannien. Trage alle unterstrichenen Informationen in die Karte ein! Put down all underlined information on the map!

Great Britain is an island. England, Wales and Scotland are parts of Great Britain. **Scotland** is in the north of the bigger island, **Wales** is in the west of the bigger island and **England** is in the east and south of the bigger island. On the right of the bigger island is the **North Sea**. Between the two islands is the **Irish Sea** and on the left is the **Atlantic (Ocean)**. In the south of England is the **English Channel**. **London** is the capital of Great Britain.

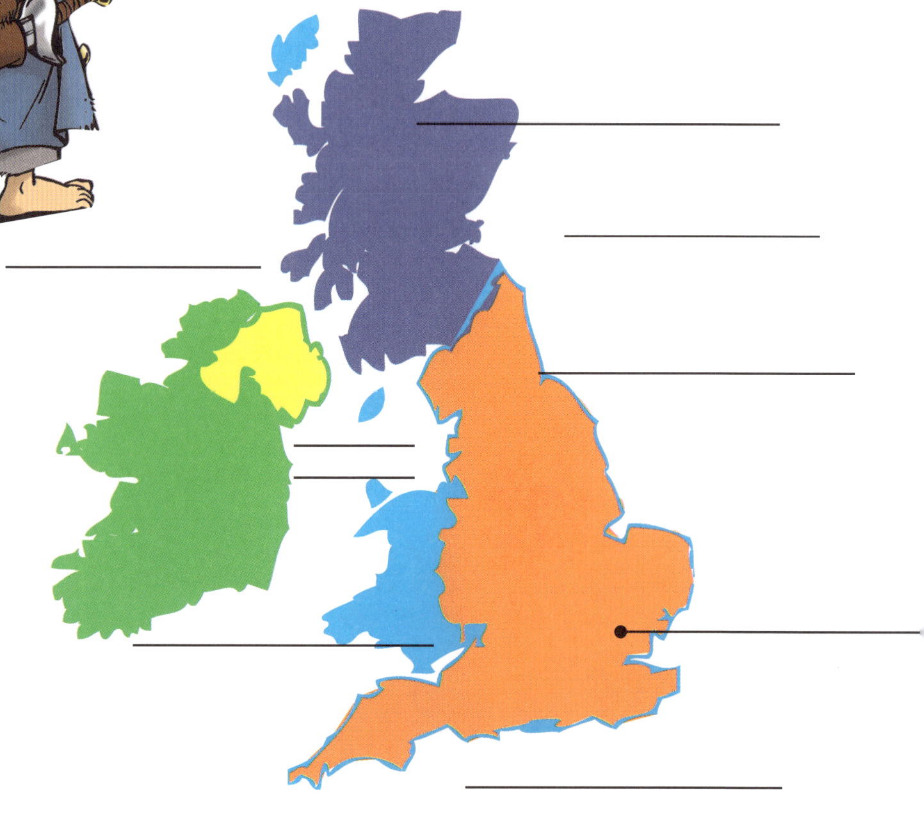

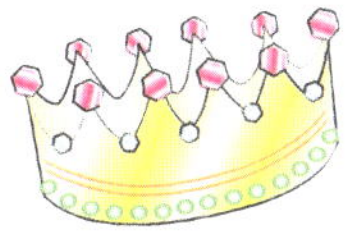

105. Aufgabe

Und kennst du auch die Abkürzung UK? UK = United Kingdom = Vereinigtes Königreich und Nordirland. Put down the information in your map!

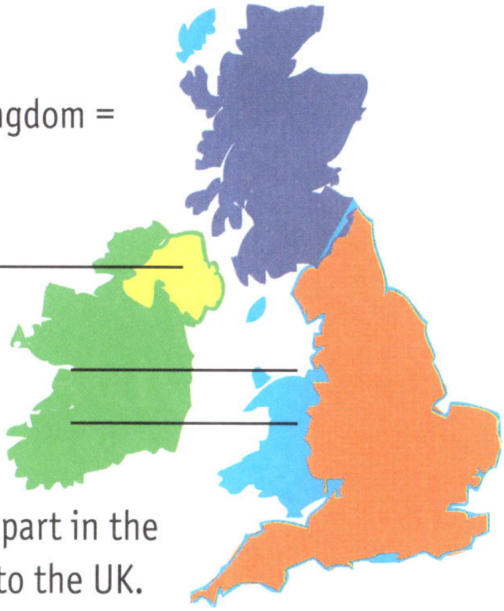

The United Kingdom is Great Britain and Northern Ireland. But there are also a number of smaller islands. On the left of Great Britain is Ireland. Ireland is an island and is **divided into** the **Republic of Ireland** and **Northern Ireland**. Northern Ireland is only a small part in the north of this island and only Northern Ireland belongs to the UK.

106. Aufgabe

Lies und übersetze anschließend! First read and then translate!

Das Königreich hat eine sehr lange und interessante Geschichte.	The United Kingdom has a very long and interesting history.
Dort gibt es viele Sehenswürdigkeiten.	There are many sights.
London ist die Hauptstadt.	London is the capital.
London ist die größte Stadt in der Europäischen Union.	London is the largest city in the European Union.
London ist älter als 1000 Jahre.	London is older than 1000 years.
London ist berühmt für seine Sehenswürdigkeiten.	London is famous for its sights.

Hauptstadt = ____________

interessant = ____________

viele = ____________

Geschichte = ____________

Sehenswürdigkeiten = ____________

dort gibt es = ____________

größte Stadt = ____________

ist älter als = ____________

ist berühmt für = ____________

Tipp

bell = Glocke
loch = scotish name for lake
Ferris wheel = Riesenrad

107. Aufgabe

Kennst du schon einige Sehenswürdigkeiten? Lies die Texte und verbinde mit den Bildern.
Do you know some sights? Read the texts and connect with the pictures!

Next to the Thames are the Houses of Parliament and beside there is a tower called Big Ben. But actually, Big Ben is a gigantic bell.

The Tower Bridge is a bridge near the Tower of London. The bridge leads over the Thames.

In Scotland, there is a dark and deep lake called Loch Ness. Some people say, there live a monster called Nessie.

In England, there are many castles and wonderful gardens. Some castles are famous for its ghosts.

Westminster Abbey is a big church in London. Almost all Kings and Queens were crowned there and buried.

The London Eye is 135 metres high and is the biggest Ferris wheel in Europe.

The most famous sight in London is the Tower of London. It is a castle with many towers and it is very old. In the middle of the Tower is the White Tower.

108. Aufgabe

Tipp
wax = Wachs

Hier sind zwei der bekanntesten Ausstellungen bzw. Museen, die Captain Clever besuchen möchte, wenn er in London ist. Here are the two best known exhibitions or museums in London! Beantworte folgende Fragen! Answer the following questions!

Madame Tussauds

Where: Marylebone Road
Underground: Baker Street
What: Tourists can see famous persons made of wax there.

Natural History Museum

Where: Cromwell Road & Exhibition Road
Underground: South Kensington
Entry: free
What: nature, plants, animals, stones, famous persons like Darwin

Where can you see films of wild animals? ____________________
What is in Marylebone Road? ____________________
Where is the entry free? ____________________
Which station is Madame Tussauds? ____________________
Where can you see the Queen? ____________________
Where can you read articles about the nature? ____________________

109. Aufgabe

Das ist typisch für Britannien und die Briten. That's typical for Britain and the British. Connect words and pictures!

9 am Faden

Gleich einem Faden reihen sich die neun Buchstaben des englischen Begriffs. Welcher Begriff ist es?

Der Begriff lautet:

____

b	r	e
s	t	a
a	f	k

Vergleichsbild

Im rechten Bild haben sich zwölf Fehler eingeschlichen. Wo stecken sie?

1. Aufgabe: Dein Regenbogen hat von unten nach oben die Farben Violett, dunkles Blau, Blau, Grün, Gelb, Orange, Rot.

2. Aufgabe: 15 grau; 99 blau; 30 gelb; 55 rot; 47 rosa; 89 grün; 100 braun; 13 lila; 72 schwarz

3. Aufgabe: Captain Clever sieht sein Schiff.

4. Aufgabe: 72 = seventy-two; 93 = ninety-three; 39 = thirty-nine; 28 = twenty-eight; 48 = forty-eight

5. Aufgabe: grey trousers = graue Hose; an eye patch = eine Augenklappe; a rapier = ein Degen; a pirate ship = ein Piratenschiff; jolly roger = Piratenflagge; an earring = ein Ohrring; a treasure map = eine Schatzkarte; a red headscarf = ein rotes Kopftuch; a treasure chest = eine Schatzkiste; a brown belt = ein brauner Gürtel; field glasses = Fernglas; a blue coat = ein blauer Mantel; an island = eine Insel; a green parrot = ein grüner Papagei

6. Aufgabe: **true:** a pirate ship, grey trousers, a green parrot, a treasure chest, an earring, a pirate flag; **false:** shoes, a yellow T-Shirt, a blue hat, a house.

7. Aufgabe: Has he got a parrot? Yes, he has. Has he got a ship? Yes, he has. Has he got an earring? Yes, he has. Has he got shoes? No, he hasn't. Has he got a treasure map? Yes, he has. Has he got a house? No, he hasn't.

8. Aufgabe: ships; apples; ducks; flowers; baskets; rabbits; maps

9. Aufgabe: 1. tomato; 2. apple; 3. pear; 4. pepper; 5. plum; 6. cucumber; 7. peach; 8. lettuce; 9. cherry; 10. grapes; 11. banana; 12. melon; 13. potato; 14. lemon; 15. carrot; 16. orange; 17. pumpkin; 18. onion; 19. bean; 20. corn

10. Aufgabe: **fruit:** plum, apple, pear, banana, grapes, melon, peach, cherry, orange, lemon; **vegetables:** pumpkin, cucumber, pepper, lettuce, onion, corn, carrot, potato, bean, tomato

11. Aufgabe: There are apples. There are onions. There is a melon. There are oranges. There is a pumpkin. There are cucumbers. There is a pepper. There is a pear.

12. Aufgabe: Are there potatoes? No, there are not. Are there oranges? Yes, there are. Are there lemons? No, there are not. Are there pears? Yes, there are. Are there onions? No, there are not.

13. Aufgabe: arm = Arm; finger = Finger; leg = Bein; hair = Haare; foot = Fuß; nose = Nase; neck = Hals; mouth = Mund; head = Kopf; knee = Knie; face = Gesicht; belly = Bauch; eye = Auge; ear = Ohr; tooth = Zahn; lips = Lippen; shoulder = Schulter; hand = Hand; back = Rücken; elbow = Ellenbogen; bottom = Po; chest = Brust

14. Aufgabe: Zeh = toe; Zahn = tooth; Zunge = tongue

15. Aufgabe: My foot hurts. My arm hurts. My back hurts. My leg hurts. My tooth hurts.

16. Aufgabe: I have a cold = Ich habe eine Erkältung. I have a temperature. = Ich habe Fieber. I am cold. = Mir ist kalt./Ich friere. I am sick/ill. = Ich bin krank.

17. Aufgabe: Get well soon! = Gute Besserung! Stay in bed! = Bleib im Bett! Take medicine! = Nimm Medizin! Go to the doctor's! = Geh zum Doktor!

18. Aufgabe:  Great. I'm very happy. Very well. I'm fine.  I'm ok. Not bad. I'm tired.  I'm ill. I'm angry.

19. Aufgabe: **Robben:** How are you? I'm happy, thanks and you? Very well. **Hund/Katze:** How are you? I'm tired and you? I'm angry. **Schildkröten:** How are you? I'm ok, thanks and you? I'm ill.

20. Aufgabe: What's your name? = Wie heißt du? Where are you from? = Woher kommst du? How old are you? = Wie alt bist du? Are you from Germany? = Bist du aus Deutschland? Which year are you in? = In welche Klasse gehst du?

21. Aufgabe: Hello, what's your name? Where are you from? How old are you? Which year are you in?

22. Aufgabe: **-ball:** basketball, volleyball, baseball, handball; **-ing:** sailing, climbing, running, riding, surfing, fishing, skiing; **other:** golf, table tennis, tennis, cricket, darts, Formula 1, athletics

23. Aufgabe: (von links nach rechts:) riding; cycling; football; fishing; sailing; running; skiing; climbing; surfing

24. Aufgabe: **Peter:** I like cycling, tennis and in-line skating. **Dave:** I like basketball, fishing and cycling. **Sue:** I like sailing, riding and swimming.

25. Aufgabe: Do you like football? Yes, I do. Do you like basketball? No, I don't. Do you like swimming? Yes, I do. Do you like riding? No, I don't. Do you like surfing? Yes, I do.

26. Aufgabe: stamp = stampfen; clap = klatschen; go = gehen; jump = springen; open = öffnen; climb = klettern; touch = berühren; play = spielen; turn around = sich drehen; shake = schütteln; close = schließen; bend = beugen

27. Aufgabe: Don't stamp with your feet. Don't play football. Don't touch the wild animals. Don't jump off the bridge. Don't go fishing. Don't open the cage. Don't swim in the lake.

29. Aufgabe: Kleid = dress; Regenjacke = rain jacket; Turnschuhe = trainers; Hose = trousers; Pullover = sweater; Bluse = blouse; Badehose = swimming trunks; Rock = skirt; Mantel = coat; Handschuhe = gloves; kurze Hose = shorts; Gürtel = belt; T-Shirt = T-shirt; Hut = hat; Stiefel = boots

30. Aufgabe: Is there a hat? Yes, there is. Is there a belt? Yes, there is. Is there a skirt? No, there is not. Is there a nightie? Yes, there is. Is there a T-shirt? Yes, there is.

31. Aufgabe: I take off my coat and put on my rain jacket. I take off my shoes and put on my trainers. I take off my trousers and put on my shorts. I take off my sweater and put on my T-shirt. I take off my swimming trunks and put on my nightie.

32. Aufgabe: belt; boots; cap; coat; dress; gloves; jacket; nightie; shirt; shoes; sweatshirt; trainers; scarf; shorts; jeans

33. Aufgabe: (von links nach rechts:) chocolate; water; ham; bacon; toast; juice; sausage; cornflakes; egg; hamburger; tea; spaghetti; jam; cake; chips; roll; pizza; meat; noodles; fish; milk; sugar; honey; ice cream; butter

34. Aufgabe: **drink:** tea, juice, lemonade, coffee, beer, milk; **eat:** meat, bread, cake, sausage, chips, cheese, buiscuit

35. Aufgabe: ~~eggs~~; ~~cake~~; ~~toast~~; ~~milk~~; ~~tomatoes~~; ~~chocolate~~; ~~coffee~~; ~~honey~~; ~~rolls~~

37. Aufgabe:

	sausages	chicken	cheese	juice	tea
Peter	☺	☺	☹	☺	☹
Sue	☹	☹	☺	☺	☺
Sally	☹	☺	☹	☺	☺

38. Aufgabe: a carton of milk = ein Karton Milch; a packet of tea = ein Päckchen Tee; a jar of jam = ein Glas Marmelade; a tin of beans = eine Büchse Bohnen; a basket of apples = ein Korb Äpfel; a bar of chocolate = eine Tafel Schokolade; a bottle of wine = eine Flasche Wein

39. Aufgabe: (von links nach rechts:) glasses; saucers; bottles; plates; bowls; cups; knives; forks; spoons; pans; pots; teapots

40. Aufgabe: 1 teapot; 2 glasses; 3 bowls; 4 bottles; 5 cups; 6 plates

41. Aufgabe: 1 = Teller; 2 = Tasse mit Untertasse; 3 = Messer und Löffel; 4 = Gabel; 5 = ein Glas Marmelade; 6 = eine große Schüssel mit Cornflakes; 7 = drei Brötchen; 8 = Käse; 9 = Zucker; 10 = ein Karton Milch; 11 = Butter; 12 = Teekanne

42. Aufgabe: meat; salt; potatoes; pepper; carrots; beans

43. Aufgabe:

G	R	E	E	N	R	F	Y	T	R	O	F
K	E	L	U	U	B	E	O	D	M	R	I
C	D	T	E	Z	L	R	M	U	A	A	F
A	Z	H	I	L	Q	B	O	Q	R	N	T
L	N	T	O	R	E	R	W	W	B	G	Y
B	K	W	P	K	B	V	T	T	N	E	Y
S	V	E	F	I	F	T	E	E	N	D	T
S	E	L	G	Z	H	X	T	N	M	R	E
I	P	V	R	E	W	U	K	H	B	Z	N
X	L	E	E	A	Z	H	N	S	G	C	I
T	N	R	Y	N	A	R	I	D	D	I	Y
Y	H	I	J	D	B	X	P	T	R	U	E
T	W	E	N	T	Y	T	H	R	E	E	J
Z	N	E	E	T	R	I	H	T	V	R	D

44. Aufgabe: 452 = four hundred and fifty-two; 743 = seven hundred and forty-three; 519 = five hundred and nineteen; 195 = one hundred and ninety-five; 245 = two hundred and forty-five; 542 = five hundred and forty-two; 347 = three hundred and forty-seven; 734 = seven hundred and thirty-four; 951 = nine hundred and fifty-one; 374 = three hundred and seventy-four; 425 = four hundred and twenty-five; 591 = five hundred and ninety-one

45. Aufgabe: cucumber; eight; bag; tree; comic; fifty; feet; parrot

46. Aufgabe: **feeling:** angry, fine, tired, sad, happy, ill; **clothes:** coat, belt, shoes, trousers, trainers, sweater; **food and drink:** spoon, juice, fork, egg, plate, chocolate, knife; **activities:** sail, jump, touch, climb, open, catch, put on; **body:** neck, knee, tooth, shoulder, leg

47. Aufgabe: (von links nach rechts:) child; children; baby; father; mother; son; daughter; parents; grandparents; grandmother; grandfather; grandchild; cousin; sister; brother; aunt; uncle; friend; familiy

48. Aufgabe: duck; Captain Clever; mouse; spider; Captain Clever; duck; sheep; spider

49. Aufgabe: Sue is Captain Clever's sister. Tom is his father. Kate is his mother. Max is his grandfather. Elia is his grandmother. Captain Clever is Bob's grandchild. Tom is Bob's son. George is Peter's uncle. Lyn is Sue's aunt. Kate is Sally's daughter.

50. Aufgabe: am; is, is; are; is, is; are; is; are; is; are

51. Aufgabe:

								C				
							P	O	S	T	E	R
		C	L	O	C	K		M				
		U						P				
M	A	P		D				U				
		B		E		B		T				
		O		S		O		E				
B	L	A	C	K	B	O	A	R	D			
I		R				K						
N		D				C						
	P	I	N	B	O	A	R	D				
						S						
				S	H	E	L	F				

52. Aufgabe: one pen; three felt tips; two rubbers; one glue; six books; two scissors; one pencil case; two rulers; one sharpener; two activity books; four markers

53. Aufgabe: Schreibe! = Write! Sprich! = Speak! Nimm! = Take! Sieh hin/an! = Look at! Lies! = Read!

54. Aufgabe: Take your scissors. Let's cut out flowers. Take your pencil. Let's draw a circle. Take your book. Let's read a story. Take your paint box. Let's paint a giraffe. Take your pen. Let's write a letter.

55. Aufgabe: Wenn du genau hinsiehst, erkennst du ein Wort: GREAT

56. Aufgabe: Can I have your pencil, please? Give me your rubber, please. Can I have your glue, please? Give me your sharpener, please. Can I have your scissors, please?

57. Aufgabe: short – long; young – old; little – big; up – down; night – day; hot – cold; happy – sad; good – bad

58. Aufgabe: January; February; March; April; May; June; July; August; September; October; November; December

59. Aufgabe: Monday; Tuesday; Wednesday; Thursday; Friday; Saturday; Sunday

60. Aufgabe: Wednesday; Thursday; Tuesday; January; February; 2009

61. Aufgabe: nine o'clock, six o'clock, twelve o'clock, ten o'clock;

62. Aufgabe: 11:00 = eleven o'clock; 3:00 = three o'clock; 7:00 = seven o'clock; 8:00 eight o'clock; 12:00 = twelve o'clock

63. Aufgabe: **1** I get up at six o'clock. **2** I wash my face and dress at half past six. **3** I have breakfast at seven o'clock. **4** I go to my pirate school at eight o'clock. **5** I go home at two o'clock in the afternoon. **6** I do my homework at four o'clock. **7** At five o'clock I play games and feed the animals. **8** I have lunch at seven o'clock in the evening. **9** I go to bed at nine o'clock.

64. Aufgabe: (von links nach rechts:) seal; shark; guinea pig; budgie; frog; ladybird; dolphin; penguin; crocodile; blackbird; owl

65. Aufgabe: EARTHWORM; TIGER; ELEPHANT; DONKEY; RABBIT; MONKEY; LION; HAMSTER; SNAIL; TURTLE; SPIDER → WILD ANIMALS

66. Aufgabe: This is a giraffe, this is a turtle, this is a sheep, this is a snail, this is a rabbit, this is a mouse and that is a lion, that is a bear, that is a horse, that is an elephant, that is a bat, that is a rhino.

67. Aufgabe: are; is; are; is; are; are; are; are; is; are

68. Aufgabe: Yes, I have. Yes, I have. Yes, I have. Yes, I have. Yes, I have. No, I haven't. No, I haven't.

69. Aufgabe:

flowers	rivers	lakes	sea	trees	jungle
jungle	trees	sea	rivers	flowers	lakes
sea	jungle	flowers	lakes	rivers	trees
trees	lakes	rivers	jungle	sea	flowers
lakes	sea	trees	flowers	jungle	rivers
rivers	flowers	jungle	trees	lakes	sea

Lösungen

70. Aufgabe: Budgies can fly. Cats can catch mice. Tigers can run. Kangaroos can jump. Fish can swim. Monkeys can climb trees. Snakes can creep. Lions can shake their body.

71. Aufgabe:

cage	left	middle	right
name	King	John	Robin
how old	12	7	9
is from	Kenia	South Africa	Tansania
likes	sleeping	catching balls	swimming

72. Aufgabe: **spring:** Easter, tulip, snowdrop; **summer:** sun, dry, sunbathing, swimming, beach, ice cream, holidays; **autumn:** kite, rain, wet, Halloween, falling leaves; **winter:** snowman, snow, cold, icy, Christmas

73. Aufgabe: rainbow – Regenbogen; temperature – warm or cold; thunderstorm – a storm with lightning; lightning – a very short light in the sky; calendar – days, months and years; forecast – what will happen next; sunshine – the light and heat of the sun; hurricane – a storm with strong wind; umbrella – Regenschirm

74. Aufgabe: Der Papagei überfliegt die gesamte Insel und kommt am Leuchtturm heraus.

75. Aufgabe:

Monday	Tuesday	Wednesday	Thursday
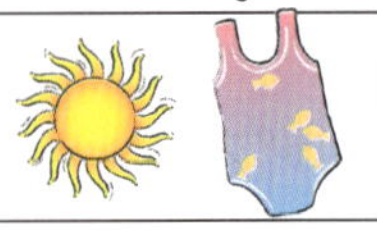			

76. Aufgabe: child – children; fish – fish; foot – feet; tooth – teeth; sheep – sheep; woman – women; leaf – leaves; knife – knives; box – boxes; peach – peaches; shelf – shelves; mouse – mice

77. Aufgabe: **month:** May, April; **nature:** tree, spider; **school:** rubber, desk; **weather:** rainbow, foggy; **family:** sister, grandmother; **nature:** rose, daffodil; **school:** write, listen to; **season:** autumn, spring; **time:** watch, clock; **animals:** bat, seal

78. Aufgabe: (von links nach rechts:) ein Baum auf der Insel; drei Fische im Netz; ein Vogel auf dem Hut; Mäuse hinter dem Schrank; Blumen zwischen den Bäumen; eine Schlange unter dem Stuhl; ein Geist neben der Uhr; ein Elefant gegenüber der Maus; ein Schneemann hinter dem Briefkasten; ein Regenbogen über der Brücke; ein Kürbis neben der Strohpuppe; die Sonne über dem Schiff

79. Aufgabe: in = darin; behind = dahinter; on = darauf; opposite = gegenüber; next to = daneben; over = darüber

80. Aufgabe: autumn; between; cage; December; Easter; foggy; German; happy; ice cream; kitchen; letter; month; night; open; present; Queen; rainbow; stamp; tomorrow; umbrella; vegetable; write; young; zebra

81. Aufgabe: Easter – Osterei; birthday – Geburtstag; New Year – Silvesterrakete; Valentine's Day – Herz; Halloween – Kürbis; Thanksgiving – Truthahn; Christmas – Weihnachtsbaum

82. Aufgabe: Happy birthday. Happy Easter. Merry Christmas. Happy New Year. Have nice holidays. Happy Thanksgiving. Trick or treat. Happy Valentine.

83. Aufgabe: 24./25. December – Christmas; 1. January – New Year; 14. February – Valentine's Day; spring – Easter; autumn – Thanksgiving

84. Aufgabe: February; December; March, April; January; die Monate, in denen du deine großen Ferien hast; dein Geburtsmonat; October, November

85. Aufgabe: chair = Stuhl; bed = Bett; table = Tisch; door = Tür; cupboard = Schrank; window = Fenster; fridge = Kühlschrank; picture = Bild; lamp = Lampe; television = Fernseher; stairs = Stufen; sofa = Sofa

86. Aufgabe: chimney = Schornstein; roof = Dach; bathroom = Badezimmer; bedroom = Schlafzimmer; living room = Wohnzimmer; stairs = Stufen; kitchen = Küche; garden = Garten

88. Aufgabe: Male: eine Maus auf dem Stuhl; eine Maus auf dem Schrank; zwei Mäuse unter dem Tisch; zwei Mäuse im Korb; eine Maus zwischen den zwei Bechern; eine Maus im Kühlschrank; zwei Mäuse hinter dem Schrank; eine Maus in einem Becher; drei Mäuse unter dem Schrank ➔ Es sind insgesamt 14 Mäuse.

89. Aufgabe: bakery; supermarket; post office; toy shop; newsagent; department store; flower shop; greengrocery

90. Aufgabe: stamps, rolls, dolls; roses, newspapers, oranges; trousers, bottles of milk, model car; comics, cakes, potatoes; card games, grapes, jar of jam

91. Aufgabe: eggs; tomatoes; butter; milk; cornflakes; orange juice; meat; chocolate

92. Aufgabe: buy; buy; pay; buy; sell; pay; sell

93. Aufgabe: **supermarket:** £ 2,00; **restaurant:** £ 3,20; **bakery:** £ 16,25; **toy shop:** £ 33,15

94. Aufgabe: £ 1,15; £ 9,75; £ 3,25; £ 3,20; £ 2,00; £ 2,50; £ 16,25; £ 33,15

95. Aufgabe: Im Norden ist ein Fußballplatz. Im Süden ist ein Spielplatz und ein Sportplatz. Im Osten sind ein Wildpark und ein Streichelzoo. Im Westen ist der Strand und ein Abenteuerspielplatz.

96. Aufgabe: **go swimming:** beach; **play football:** soccer pitch, sports field; **ride ponies:** children's zoo; **feed the animals:** children's zoo; **go climbing:** playground; **play ball:** playground, soccer pitch, sports field, beach; **go sailing:** beach; **make sand castles:** playground, beach

97. Aufgabe: Steven – soccer pitch; Captain Clever – playground; Anne – beach; Peter – park for wild animals; Tom – children's zoo; Sue – park for wild animals

98. Aufgabe: Du beginnst am Schiff, kletterst über die Berge, springst über den Fluss, gehst durch den Wald, schwimmst über den See, gehst den Strand entlang, gehst über die Brücke und reitest zum Abenteuerspielplatz.

99. Aufgabe: spaceship = Raumschiff; bus = Bus; racing car = Rennauto; sailing boat = Segelboot; lorry = LKW; motorbike = Motorrad; bike = Fahrrad; helicopter = Hubschrauber; U-Bahn = underground; tractor = Traktor; plane = Flugzeug; train = Zug; alleine steht: rocket = Rakete

100. Aufgabe: **Great Britain:** by ship, by plane, by train; **Australia:** by plane; **Berlin:** by train, by car, by bus; **USA:** by plane

101. Aufgabe: bus – bus stop; train – station; plane – airport; ship – harbour; taxi – taxi stop

102. Aufgabe: bus stop; station; airport; taxi stop

103. Aufgabe: £ – pound, penny (pence) –  ; € – euro, cent –  ; $ – dollar, cent – 

104. Aufgabe:

105. Aufgabe:

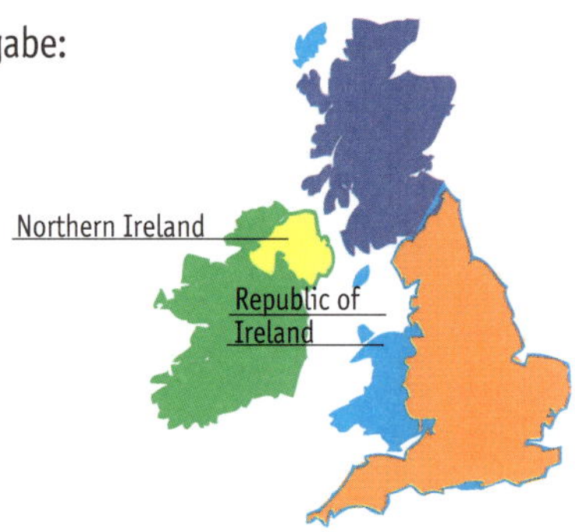

106. Aufgabe: interessant = interesting; Sehenswürdigkeiten = sights; viele = many; Hauptstadt = capital; Geschichte = history; dort gibt es = there are; größte Stadt = largest city; ist älter als = is older than; ist berühmt für = is famous for

107. Aufgabe:  Tower Bridge;  Houses of Parliament;

 Big Ben;  castle and garden; 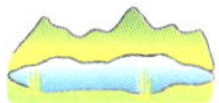 Loch Ness;

 Westminster Abbey;  London Eye;  Tower

108. Aufgabe: Natural History Museum; Madame Tussauds; Natural History Museum; Baker Street; Madame Tussauds; Natural History Museum

109. Aufgabe: a red letter box = ein roter Briefkasten; rainy days = verregnete Tage; fish and chips = Fisch und Pommes; tea time = Teestunde; a red phone box = eine rote Telefonzelle

Riddles

S. 11: Gleiche suchen: Nr. 3 und 5

Punktebild: Schiff

S. 16: Vergleichsbild:

4 am Faden: body

S. 22: Labyrinth:

Was ist das?: Hasenfuß

S. 27: Schattenriss: Nr. 5

Rebus: ~~En~~gel; D~~ach~~; ~~Bi~~b~~er~~; Eu~~le~~; Tel~~efon~~ → Geldbeutel

S. 34: Vergleichsbild:

Umrissbild: Nr. 3

S. 41: Gleiche suchen: Nr. 3 und 4

S. 49: Was ist das? Zaunkönig

Labyrinth:

S. 56: Vergleichsbild:

Englisches Rebus: ~~c~~a~~t~~; ni~~ne~~; m~~ouse~~; ~~b~~al~~l~~ → animal

S. 63: Schattenriss: Nr. 4

Punktebild: Hund

S. 70: 9 am Faden: breakfast

Vergleichsbild: